T0355039

MORE TALES
FROM
THE
YARD

OTHER BOOKS BY JAMES R. PALMER

DOING TIME EIGHT HOURS A DAY
MEMOIRS OF A CORRECTIONAL OFFICER

MORE TALES
FROM
THE
YARD

STORIES
FROM INSIDE
THE PRISON

Memoirs of a Correctional Officer

JAMES R. PALMER

MORE TALES FROM THE YARD
STORIES FROM INSIDE THE PRISON
MEMOIRS OF A CORRECTIONAL OFFICER

Copyright © 2024 James R. Palmer.

All rights reserved. No part of this book may be used or reproduced by any means, graphic, electronic, or mechanical, including photocopying, recording, taping or by any information storage retrieval system without the written permission of the author except in the case of brief quotations embodied in critical articles and reviews.

The names of the Officers or inmates described in these stories have been changed or eliminated. This is for their protection, as some may still be there doing time, either as an Officer or an inmate.

iUniverse books may be ordered through booksellers or by contacting:

iUniverse
1663 Liberty Drive
Bloomington, IN 47403
www.iuniverse.com
844-349-9409

Because of the dynamic nature of the Internet, any web addresses or links contained in this book may have changed since publication and may no longer be valid. The views expressed in this work are solely those of the author and do not necessarily reflect the views of the publisher, and the publisher hereby disclaims any responsibility for them.

Any people depicted in stock imagery provided by Getty Images are models, and such images are being used for illustrative purposes only. Certain stock imagery © Getty Images.

ISBN: 978-1-6632-6811-2 (sc)
ISBN: 978-1-6632-6813-6 (hc)
ISBN: 978-1-6632-6812-9 (e)

Library of Congress Control Number: 2024922161

Print information available on the last page.

iUniverse rev. date: 11/27/2024

Contents

Contents

About the Author

The author, James R. Palmer, spent twenty years serving his country in the military. He then spent several years in the corporate world before joining the Department of Corrections in Kentucky. He spent his entire career at (LLCC) Luther Luckett Correctional Complex.

He was also an FBI-trained hostage negotiator.

Now retired, he still resides in Kentucky.

These two books were written because he wanted to provide the uninformed a glimpse of what happens inside those four walls of either concrete or chain link fence and razor wire. To get a feel of what it's like to be 'incarcerated' with some of society's worst and some not quite so bad. A chance to read about the stories of some of the things that transpire inside. Those who retired from the DOC always said they would write a book, but none ever did. So, he did. The first book, Doing Time Eight Hours a Day: Memoirs of a Correction Officer, was published several years ago. This is the sequel: More Tales from the Yard, Stories from Inside the Prison.

Here it is, please enjoy.

Dedication

Again, thank you to my wife, Donna, who puts up with my whims. Thanks, Bud. I love you.

This book is also dedicated to James and Amelia for their technical assistance and the long, late-night phone calls. Thank you. I love you.

And to all Correctional Officers and Jailers who do these jobs in a professional manner twenty-four seven, three hundred sixty-five days a year. Stay safe and trust your gut feeling. It's usually not wrong!

And lastly, in memory of Jim (Ollie) Oliver.

Cover photo courtesy of Andy Floyd

C/O Extraordinaire

The Prison Version of The Miranda Warning

You have the right to swing first. However, if you choose to swing first, any move you make can and will be used as an excuse to beat the shit out of you. You have the right to have a doctor and a priest present. If you cannot afford a doctor or are not presently attending a church of your choice, one will be appointed to you.

Do you understand what I just told you, asshole?

This is a joke version of the original Miranda warning, used only for our internal amusement and use. It is not intended to replace the original version used by law enforcement.

After all, we need some humor, too!

The Correctional Officers Prayer

Lord, when it's time to go inside,
That place of steel and stone,
I pray that you will keep me safe,
So I won't walk alone.

Help me to do my duty.

Please watch over me in my rounds.

Amongst those perilous places
And slamming steel door sounds.

God, keep my fellow officers
Well, and free from harm.

Let them know I'll be there too,
Whenever there's an alarm.

Above all, when I walk my beat,
No matter where I roam,
Let me go back whence I came
To family and home.

With thanks and appreciation to:
Larry Peoples (Lt.) Ret. Florida Dept. Of Corrections

Some of the Abbreviations We Used

AA/NA	Alcoholics Anonymous/Narcotics Anonymous
ARNP	Advanced Registered Nurse Practitioner
CI	Confidential Informant
CPR	Cardio-Pulmonary Resuscitation
CTO	Classification and Treatment Officer. Nonuniform staff for the inmates to go to in the dorms for a variety of things.
DOC	Department of Corrections
GED	General Education Development
IA	Internal Affairs
KCIW	Kentucky Correctional Institute for Women
KCPC	Kentucky Correctional Psychiatric Center
KSP	Kentucky State Police
KSP	Kentucky State Penitentiary
KSR	Kentucky State Reformatory
LLCC	Luther Luckett Correctional Complex
PC	Protective Custody (Prison Chicken)
RCC	Roederer Correctional Complex
SEG	Segregation
SOTP	Sex Offender Treatment Program
TAD	Transportation, Admissions and Discharge

TIME

NOTHING TO DO BUT TIME

TIME is slow when you wait.
TIME is fast when you're late.
TIME is deadly when you're sad.
TIME is short when you're happy.
TIME is endless when you're in pain.
TIME is long when you're bored.

Everything is determined by your feelings and psychological conditions, NOT by the clock.

It's a funny thing; everybody assumes that they have an abundance of time left to do whatever they want to do. However, we never know what tomorrow will bring. Here today, gone tomorrow. Life is short. Here is something to think about:

THE MOMENT WE ARE BORN IS THE MOMENT WE BEGIN TO DIE!

Ponder that for a minute...

Time is short. Life is short. Much shorter than you think.

Money can't buy it. You can't earn more of it, bank it, or save it up for later. Once it's gone... it's gone. Forever. TIME... Time...Time... Time...Tick Tock. Tick Tock. It just fades away.

It's all about time. Put it to good use. Don't waste it! Use it wisely. The biggest mistake we make is thinking we have more time. Time expires when we least expect it.

As the days go by, everything you do becomes so much more monotonous. This can be easily seen in the endless, mundane days of nothingness, doing nothing but the same old nothing each and every day. Not going to the supermarket or the department store. No big box stores. No restaurants or fast-food places. No shopping with the kids for new school clothes. No new clothes or shoes for yourself. Just state-issued. Soon you think, 'What can I do today that will be different from yesterday, today, or tomorrow that will help pass the time, the time of this damn boredom that I am now saddled with'? Not much comes to mind.

As one's mind begins to wander and you're thinking about that, you start thinking back to the good old days, the days before you were here, when things went awry, you and your family's lives were forever turned upside down, caused by some stupid things that you've done, the days before being incarcerated here in prison. In the days before this nightmare became a living reality, this existence became a multi-year torment for everyone and a misery of existence within these bars, walls, and fences. The walls of your dorm. Your room. Your home. Everything is painted one drab color that never changes, even if you want it to. The fences of this prison, or of any other prison that you have created, this hell hole that you will be calling home for the next how many years, if not forever?

Well...what if...WHAT IF? How many times have you said this to yourself? So many thoughts often cross one's mind. Remembering and reliving the happier days and times, well those days are gone now. Beautiful sun-filled days frolicking with the kids, grandkids, grandparents, wife, parents, and old friends at the swimming pool, backyard BBQs, and brews. Now, with nothing but endless time to dwell on, to think of the outside, the past, to be ANYWHERE but here. Close your eyes and contemplate that for a minute. What would have been? What should have been? What could have been? All it would have taken was just a dab of common sense, some backbone to say no to the temptation and friends that put you here. Maybe they are here or at another facility, too. But you knew better. A quick buck, some free merchandise, or maybe a buzz that didn't last that long.

Outside these walls and the fences topped with endless row after row of barbed or razor wire are the family and friends that you won't be seeing for extended periods — if at all for some... never except on those rare visiting days once a week and an occasional holiday when your family and friends make it up to see you. Those who were your "close" friends, your BFFs, are now mostly fading memories that you hope and pray will stay in touch. After all, you are now gone from their everyday lives and normal routines, yet life must still carry on doing what everyone does. Going to restaurants and shopping at malls. Burgers, fries, onion rings. Malts and shakes and other things. It's their routine now. Not yours. It's their time. Not yours. Your time is doing time.

3

Maybe you will get two or three letters a week telling you what's up at home, work, school, or the job you used to have. Or the occasional COLLECT phone call you make, hoping that whoever you call will accept that call and can or will pay the charges. It can get expensive depending on how often you call. The latest new (old) gossip you used to get daily when you were back home on the street with your old friends and family, but now you are gone. Almost forgotten. Time is fading the memory. All of your old friends are fading as you are fading from the recesses of their minds and thoughts. Seldom thought of, if at all. It's a fact. After all, you are in prison, not them, so to speak. But your family and friends are also in a prison...a prison of their own that you built to give to everyone. YOU put your friends and family there. Suddenly, you are gone. You are not there every day to see the folks talk face to face and listen to their problems, as they, in turn, listen to yours. To be able to give advice to your kids, probably the same advice you got and didn't listen to, to encourage them in difficult learning endeavors, school activities, recitals, plays, sports, never to watch the youngsters play a football or baseball or basketball game—for how long? All the everyday mundane activities you got bored with doing every day at home, the sometimes made-up lame-ass excuses you used to not attend, those things you can't do now but yearn to. This brings back the memories; those memories cause great angst because you are not able to console your family and friends in the hard times and praise them in the good. Now, the closeness you once shared is not there anymore. Close but not so much anymore, even though you were "runnin' buddies" maybe at one time or a partner in crime, as the saying goes. Everyone promised you a lot when

4

you left, all kinds of support for you and your family. But as time goes by, those promises keep slipping away because their lives go on, as does yours, but in totally different worlds. Now that you are gone, these people have their own lives to lead, their families to watch over and raise the kids, maybe even yours.

Their normal routine goes on. After all, when you got sentenced, there were promises made, sworn to keep. The money would be sent, money that is desperately needed and wanted by you on the inside for your canteen. Using that canteen to eat or as money for your debts, even in some cases protection, your livelihood, your existence. But now it is also needed by your friends and family for THEIR livelihood, THEIR existence, to pay THEIR bills, gas for the car to come to see you, food, and overnight hotel lodging if the drive is far enough. So, your money gets cut a little at a time until it's almost down to nothing, yet you keep asking for more. Your job here isn't going to put you in a millionaires' row, but it's somewhere between having nothing and maybe one dollar and eighty-five cents per hour if you're lucky enough to get one of the great jobs.

On visiting days, it's only a couple of hours of relief to see those family and friends who can come, and only four people can sit at a table. Eating a day- or week-old sandwich purchased from a machine, zapped in the microwave with a bag of chips, a soda purchased with the twenty dollars cash they are allowed to bring, in change only. The visit is short, usually only two hours, to catch up on the happenings and events at home. In some cases, pass on information that can't be written down or spoken over the phone. Yes, crime continues on the inside. It never stops. Thinking of what might have been.

5

Thinking of what could have been. Thinking of what should have been... Just thinking. Take a look around at everything, at nothing, at the same thing, every day, day after day, month after month, year after year, knowing that this is what it is that you are going to see for the next five, ten, or twenty years or more or in some cases... LIFE. LIFE. How long is that?? Christmas Day. Thanksgiving Day. Your birthday. Their birthdays. Anniversaries. Births. Deaths. Funerals. Weddings. Both happy and sad events. You will hear about them and perhaps see a few photos of those events, but it's not the same as being there in person; time comes, time goes.

Nothing to do but walk the yard, walk the recreation field loop, go to the weight pile and handball court, walk the walkway, and wear down your shoe leather. If you have a job, you go there, then go "home" to the dorm. Eat dinner and watch some TV. Do it again. Tomorrow and tomorrow and yet again tomorrow... Endless years of nothingness. What a waste. The view will only change if or when you get a transfer. Oh, you will get transferred to another facility, where you have probably been there and done that before, so the view never changes. The people change. The view doesn't. The time continues no matter where you go or what you are doing. In-state or out-state. Time waits for no man.

With all this time on your hands, you have to make a plan for when your time is up. Having a plan and something to look forward to when you go home is important because old habits are hard to break. Without a plan, you're more likely to return. If you fail to plan, you plan to fail.

YOU DID THE CRIME...
NOW YOU GOTTA DO THE TIME

Going to prison for the first time? Nothing is so painful to the human psyche as great or sudden change. We all resist change. But change is inevitable. We all have to change with it. Learn to bend with it or break against it.

There is a learning curve in everything we do in life. We may know what to do and how to do it in all of what we are doing. However, in all situations, we have to learn many of the particular nuances of a specific job or task that we are embarking on. Knowing ahead of time what to do or what to expect makes the transition a whole lot easier and less troublesome. A smooth transition. The same goes in prison. Ok. You did the crime; now you gotta do the time.

For the first-timers, going to the penitentiary can be a scary thing. The penitentiary is very different from the county jail you just left. It's bigger, scarier, and far more intimidating. So are the people there. If you did something before or spent some time in jail, you have a feeling of what to expect, but

THIS is different. What to do. What not to do. When to do it. What to expect. How am I going to survive? Below is a small list of things you need to know. To help keep your ass out of trouble, keep you from getting prison justice imposed upon you. Although this list is not all-encompassing, it is full of good information. I'm sure other folks have a list of their own that pertains to a particular institution. Still, these are some of the most basic...that can help you survive... until you learn the prison way of life, or at least help to get you through your time inside. Hopefully, these will keep you from getting your ass kicked, also known as prison justice or a tune-up. Each institution has its own "ground rules," and the people who enforce these both written and unwritten rules. You quickly need to learn them all as time goes by. Also, someone will be there to help acclimate you to these rules. Of course, the unwritten yard rules are not published or written anywhere.

There is no printed rule book, just an unwritten guide, usually passed on to the new "fish" to help you get used to your new surroundings. It's "free" advice but comes with a price that will be collected later. Remember, nothing is free in prison. It's the unwritten rules that you need to concern yourself with. These are the ones that will save you a lot of trouble, some fights, maybe some ass whoopin'. Hopefully by watching and observing, just don't ask too many questions. You might be trying to learn, but others may take that as being nosy. You need to learn these unofficial rules to get along before you get "approached" and get taught before you get punched in the face for being a wise guy or a smart ass. But it's mostly common sense. Only sometimes, in prison, it's not so common! Here are some common-sense things to know and follow. It seems like a long list, but there are many for each different prison. And they'll help you out in the day-to-day life inside.

1. **Mind your own business.**

   As it is commonly said today, stay in your lane. Just like it says. Unless you are asked, it doesn't include or concern you. You mind your business, I'll mind mine, and everyone will get along fine.

2. **Mind your place.**

   In the weight room, TV room, game room, or pool room, wait your turn. It's like the bar room or old pool hall back home. You put up your quarter for a game and then wait your turn to play. Except here, there are no quarters.

3. **Wait your turn.**

   In the chow hall, canteen, pill call, medical, or shower lines, don't cut the line even if someone lets you. Those behind you in line may not understand, nor will they care. More altercations start over this than just about any other thing in prison.

4. **Knock. Even if it's your room.**

   Especially if the door is closed or the cell door window is covered, it's private time. Even a prearranged signal, such as something hanging on the door handle, makes it private time for the people inside. It may be the toilets, your room, or something sexual that is going on, either alone or with someone else. Yes, it does happen in prison. Stay out. Everyone needs or deserves a little alone time.

5. Take care of your hygiene.

Nobody likes a stinker. Clean up after yourself, your room, your bedding, and your area. You don't want a cleaning party to visit you in the middle of the night, encouraging you to clean up. In the Army, these were called GI parties. Not very pleasant, but it got the job done, and it got the point across. Take that shower. A lot. The water is free.

6. Don't touch.

If you didn't put it there, it's not yours. Don't touch it. Leave it alone. It could have been placed there as a trap to test you. Personal items, food, drink, snacks, mail. Especially mail. More especially legal mail.

7. Pay your debts. Or better yet - don't incur any.

Always pay your debts promptly if you get any. But try to avoid incurring any debts. Everything in prison costs. As does everything that is "free". Haircuts, laundry, etc. That is how things work in prison. Nobody likes a swindler or a person who doesn't honor his debts. Paying your bills keeps you out of trouble and keeps you healthy. It establishes your reputation that you are trusted or can be trusted. After all, look who you are surrounded by. Not all of these people are the world's finest upstanding citizens. In prison, a man has two things: his word and his reputation. Without these, he has nothing, and among the rest of the inmates, that is a lot!

8. Don't disrupt or interrupt.

Whether it's a nap, a card game, or a board game unless you are asked. You don't know what's on the line. Hmmm. It could be another bet on a card or a domino game. Say it ain't so.

9. Stay in your area.

In a cell with two people, it's hard to get confused; but stay off your cellmate's bunk. Even in a common area or a large sleeping area, stay in your assigned space.

10. Respect

Give it to receive it. Both to the officers and inmates. But don't be a suck-up. Officers and inmates can tell the difference. Respect, it goes a long way.

11. Stay away.

When stuff happens, get away and stay away. Don't get involved. You could be getting into something more than you expect or are prepared to handle. Walk away, but don't run. It makes you look guilty.

12. Keep your hands to yourself.

Don't touch another inmate. NO MATTER WHAT. Don't reach across another's food plate in the chow hall for anything. Ask for whatever you're reaching for, even the salt and pepper.

13. Don't lie.

Remember, there's always a paper trail. Anyone can call home and have someone look up on the computer what you're in for with all the details of your crime. Computers and newspapers are everywhere, even in prison. Lies get called out. Every time you lie, you create problems that you will have to deal with later on in the future. Do the right thing.

14. Mind your manners.

Saying "please" and "thank you" can go a long way to staff members and other inmates, even in prison. It goes along with RESPECT. (See above.)

15. Don't steal.

Everyone has very little in prison and nobody wants to lose that. The little bit of stuff they do have, if you get caught stealing it, you will get instant retaliation and a bad reputation.

16. Don't stare.

Staring can mean a challenge or that you're looking for a close "friend."

17. Don't be nosy.

Keep to yourself if you can. Take care of YOUR business and leave the others alone.

18. Don't sag.

Sagging your britches is the prison way of flirting. It also says what you are looking for. Up here—down there. Everyone is watching for whom you sag. It could invite more than trouble. People get jealous. Beware the green-eyed monster.

19. Don't brag.

Either about what you had out there, what you did out there, or what you have in here. It's easy to get checked up on. It will come back to haunt you.

20. Don't discuss your crime.

Especially if it's a sex crime. You should even consider protective custody if it's a sex crime against kids or older people.

21. Don't befriend the guards.

Do your business when you have to, but don't get friendly. The rest of the inmates will think you're getting 'snitchy'. Or you're looking for favors.

22. Don't make every inmate your friend.

Some will want to be your friend. Choose them wisely.

23. Don't abuse your phone privileges.

Someone else wants to use the phone, too.

24. Don't be loud after dark or lights out.

Others want to rest, sleep, or watch a little TV. Sleep is very important in prison. Everyone wants it.

25. Keep healthy both physically, mentally, spiritually. It's for your healthy disposition.

26. Do not tell everyone you're innocent, especially if you are not. It can be checked.

27. Don't show others how afraid you really are.

Remember, everyone was that way once upon a time.

28. Don't mess with somebody else's 'bitch or punk.'

29. Three things not to discuss. Sex, politics, religion.

Remember those three monkeys? Hear no evil, see no evil, speak no evil?

BE LIKE A MONKEY.

The bottom line is MYOB. Mind your own business.

The last thing to remember is: SNITCHES GET STITCHES. ALWAYS.

There are many more that could be added to this list; each prison has its own list. Learn these rules fast and keep to yourself. Shut up, watch, and learn.

After you make a mistake, life goes on. But sometimes, you keep kicking yourself. In other words, you have voluntarily chosen a life sentence for a poor decision you made in the past. NOW is the time to appeal that decision. Resolve to commute that emotional sentence to make amends with yourself, and declare that you will not spend another minute of another day reliving a decision that cannot be changed. Move on!

After all, the windshield is more significant than the rearview mirror because we need to see where we are going, not where we've been.

THINGS TO DO

Now that you're here (in prison), you have to learn to keep yourself busy. It's great for your mind, spirit, and body. Doing nothing all day is detrimental to you and those around you. It also fosters resentment and hard feelings. Find things to do, including getting a job. That will put money in your account, making you less dependent on those family and friends outside. After all, they need money, too. And it'll definitely help pass the time, make it go faster, and improve your outlook for the future in prison, however long that will be.

Life in prison is full of resentment and that might be because of the guilt or a sense of a task left unaccomplished or unfulfilled. It might sound strange to talk about things to do in prison as if it were a holiday or a retreat for an opportunity. It's a punishment for wrong acts or acts committed.

Inside these walls, it's like the line from the old prison movie, "get busy living or get busy dying." The time will go faster if you have something to do to occupy your mind and your time. It will even help keep you out of trouble. Time, don't waste it. Use it to go to school, finish your GED, get some college, or complete your degree. A Bachelor's, Master's, or a PhD, depending on time. Remember, it's not impossible. After all, you've got a bunch of time to do it. Many inmates have done it, plus the tuition can't be beat. Besides, what else have you got to do? Make your family proud, and set an example so your kids don't end up where you are. Here's your opportunity to get a skill, learn a career or a trade. Make something of yourself for when you get out. Improve yourself. If not for anybody else, do it for yourself.

The days vary for each individual. Some have jobs. Some go to school; some attend trade school in prison: plumbing, carpentry, auto mechanics, and data entry are just a few that are offered. Each prison offers its own trade schools. There are also court-mandated classes that must be attended as a prerequisite to seeing the parole board. AA, Alcoholics Anonymous, NA, Narcotics Anonymous, SOTP, and Sex Offender Treatment Program are just a few. So, some of your time is going to be preprogrammed for you. Now, it's up to you to make things better for yourself and your family. Many people take up arts and crafts or drawing as something to do with their idle time, especially at night in your room. Be creative. You would be surprised what's inside you.

The law library is usually very busy for those who think or hope they might get or should get a new trial or appeal of their case. Of course, your attorneys are also looking into your crime. Still, the inmate has all the time in the world to look for something to overturn their verdict or hopefully get a new trial. It's a long, slow process, but it's something to do. Some jailhouse lawyers were good at it. Some would even help you on your case, for a fee, of course, when not working on their own case. Some were good; some, not so much. I guess that's where the term shit house lawyers came from.

There was one inmate who worked long and hard on his appeal for years. Yes, it does take that long. He finally got a new trial, and he eventually won his case. He got his conviction overturned, and his legal research work was so good that he impressed his legal team. So, when he was released, the law firm that he had hired to defend him, offered him a job as a legal researcher. His was the exception, not the rule. He was determined to succeed and persevere, which he did. The last I knew of him, he was still at that legal firm doing good things for other inmates.

Some people try to better themselves before being released. Others wander the yard, moseying around doing nothing but then, doing nothing is doing. They might be trying to think of ways to beat the system, get ahead, or make a few "dollars", i.e., Prison Money: food, stamps, or snacks. It's just passing time until everyone understands that everyone needs something to do to pass that time and make the time go faster. After all, the parole board could be years away, if at all, then the board will look at your record to see what you've been doing with your time. Have you been productive or just wasting time?

The officers working there, especially those assigned to the dorms on a permanent basis, notice the change in your behavior and your normal life cycle. After all, prison is now your normal cycle of life. The inmates are, just like the rest of us, only some are incarcerated for things that their friends may have talked them into doing back home, they acted on the spur of the moment, went along with the crowd, or just wanted to be part of things. In everyone's lives, there are or were things that could have gotten some people in as much trouble as the convicts here, but something prevented that. It was something called a conscience that got the better of us, or maybe we were shown some leniency by someone along the way. Maybe someone had enough influence to encourage positive decisions instead of harmful ones. Even the first, and hopefully one-time, offender who might have committed a heinous crime or a crime that could have gotten anyone locked up had that moment that could have made a difference. Some criminals are truly sorry, but we all must remember that everyone here is still a human. To be treated with a firm, fair, and consistent hand.

While in prison, you will meet a lot of people. An inmate will become friends with some, if not many, of them. Choose your friends wisely because you'll likely meet up with some of these guys or gals later after you get out. These people may become an influence in your life, so maybe it's time to decide whether to let them in or not. It could be a positive influence. Maybe that influence could be bad, leading to another stretch away from home and your loved ones. Then you'll be back seeing some of your good old friends again. Never forget that some of your 'friends' will drop you because you're in prison. Surround yourself with a positive influence to better yourself.

Here are some other ways prisoners kill or pass the time while in prison:

They sleep. A lot. If you don't have a daily schedule or a job that takes up most of your day, sleep inevitably takes up a lot of your time. Sleeping all the time does make you tired, and when you're tired, you sleep. It can become a vicious cycle.

They work out. If not in the gym or weight pile, they use whatever they have to make weights: Books tied together and water in plastic trash bags. Remember, one gallon of water equals eight pounds, so it adds up to a lot of weight.

They watch TV a lot. Most prisons encourage you to get "out" and find things to do in a constructive way, so they have rules about staying in your room all day. TV watching can become boring, but for those with nothing to do, it is all time-consuming.

Writing letters is very popular and important as inmates try to reconnect with those from the past whom they haven't heard from in a while. Also, they are hoping to get mail in return.

They learn to play games—not only the prison kind but board games like chess. There are many chess masters in prison who are happy to teach you how to play. Checkers and dominoes are extremely popular, but most people already know how to play these games.

They gamble—on anything. Although they may not be large bets, it's the thrill of the bet that matters. It's about bragging rights. Even though gambling is prohibited, it's hard to catch them at it, much less prove it.

Reading books is also a big pastime. Some inmates read everything they can get their hands on, and for some, it even inspires them to try their hand at writing.

Many books have been written by inmates, some while in prison and some after they got out. Many of these books are pretty informative. The books they write usually contain a more detailed or inclusive list of dos and don'ts. They also give hints that are usually kept among the inmates—except now.

Making arts and crafts is very popular with many inmates; it gives them something to do to pass the time. This can be done in the gym, the arts and crafts room, or back in your dorm.

Your room or the dorm's common area are two more good places, as some don't need peace or quiet, and some collaborate when working together. Swap ideas and help mentor each other. Using things like popsicle sticks and wooden matches, some inmates become very creative in what they make. Some of the most popular items are decorative jewelry cases, intricate cigarette cases, or small boxes to hold knick-knacks. When these are completed, they mail them home to family or friends. Some prisons even have a program where they can be sold to other visitors or staff. The money then goes into their account so they are not as dependent on their family.

WHAT WERE THEY THINKING?

Different people do different things at the strangest of times. If you watch people long enough, the tells that are given off usually give themselves away. Then, it's just a matter of slowly putting pieces together.

One afternoon, I was working a tower while watching a softball game on the recreation field. Watching both the inmates as well as well as the ball game all at the same time. Multi-tasking, I guess. One dorm versus another. There were some great ball players on both teams. Surprisingly, the games were usually good. There were a lot of young, healthy, athletic inmates in prison, and it also helped to pass the time. The exercise was good for those who wanted to stay in shape, so when it was time to play, they did play hard. The more these games were played, the less likely 'inmate games' were played. As things went on in prison, there had to be some wager on the outcome. Stamps, canteen, ramen noodles, honey buns, chips, soda, or various canned goods. All the usual prison currency.

I noticed three individuals off the right field foul line during the game. It was apparent that these three musketeers weren't trying to hide anything that was going on. In fact, it looked almost normal just walking around. But then I noticed that something was a little bit amiss. These three inmates were taking "giant steps" as they paced off distances from different points of the ball field to different points of the walkway close to the inner fence. There was also an outer fence beyond that, that they looked at for reference points. The distance between the two fences was about twenty-five feet. But then there would be some guessing as to the distances to the fences in areas that were off limits.

Both fences were topped off with at least four strands of razor wire. But as these guys were pacing things off, going almost unnoticed, one was jotting down distance notes from point A to point B, and the third inmate relayed the information. All fences are off-limits to inmates, and there are signs posted on the fences that deadly force is enforced.

But what was so interesting in all that? I notified the Yard Lieutenant of what I was watching and who was involved. I recognized the individuals from the times that I worked in the dorms on many previous occasions. And some guys always stick out because they are usually up to something, so they become well-known to the guards. These three were always scheming or up to something nefarious. Trying to con the cons and con the staff members to get something for nothing. The Lieutenant responded with several officers and found these characters close to the outfield foul poles. The responding officers conducted a frisk search of these three characters, who were identified, confiscated the papers that they had concealed, and then escorted them back to their respective dorms, where the inmates had their cells thoroughly searched. At the dorms, the officers, along with the Lieutenant, conducted searches and found several different pieces of maps with distances from points A to B to C from different areas of the yard that were accessible to most inmates. Other areas of the prison yard measured distances could only have been obtained by maintenance inmates. The information found included some drawings along with detailed notes. These could only have been passed on for a price, I suppose, since they were from restricted areas. But asking who gave it to them would be useless because these guys always remembered that snitches get stitches.

Not knowing who their contacts were, it was hard to accuse much less incriminate anyone. However, after the cell searches were concluded, these three were locked up in segregation in different wings to limit access to each other. Some maps were in areas where the information could only be obtained by maintenance inmates being escorted to their jobs. Even then, the information could get passed in the mail, but most mail between inmates was opened, monitored, and read. Still, in prison, information always found a way to get sent in or out.

It must have been a daunting task that had been in the works for several weeks, if not months, and, if everything went according to plan, even harder to carry out. Needless to say, their transfers were completed about two days later. They were all sent to various parts of the state furthest away from their families or visiting friends with instructions not to visit for six months, with all phone calls recorded and monitored.

There are other inmates who just need something to do with their time, so they become innovative entrepreneurs. They use wet toilet paper to make a pair of dice. Keep it wet; keep it square until it dries, and then it becomes hard. Put the dots on them with ink from the print shop or use an ink pen, and you have a pair of dice. They are easy to flush when needed and readily available to make another.

While in prison, assaulting a staff member is a sure way to get a transfer if that's what you're looking for. Just try to remember that the next place may be worse than the one you're at now. And it could be even farther down the road for your family to visit. And more charges will definitely come.

One case in point was when an inmate working in the prison print shop used an exacto knife as one of his working tools. It was properly signed out and accounted for each hour, so no alarms were triggered when he had it. When a female staff was going to use the staff restroom, he followed her to the door, and before she could enter and lock it, he pushed his way in and showed her the knife. She screamed, and another staff member heard it and activated the alarm button. This button activated an alarm and a red light on the building. But before any staff could respond, another inmate intervened on her behalf and took down the assailant. The two inmates wrestled on the floor as staff responded (I was the second to enter). We broke up the fight and put the two individuals in cuffs because we didn't know what happened or what was going on with the inmates who were fighting. The female staff was hysterical, and she was escorted to medical to be evaluated and calmed down. The two inmates were kept separated until the Shift Captain and Yard Supervisor arrived and took over the investigation, which lasted several hours. It was eventually determined what happened and it was clear that one inmate had actually helped out the female staff. He was put in segregation for his protection as the investigation continued. The other, who did the assault, was transferred to KSP, the maximum-security prison that night, under the guard of a Lieutenant and two officers. The assailant was subsequently tried and convicted of his assault, resulting in an additional ten years added to his sentence. But that was no matter as he was doing life for the same type of crime on the outside.

The inmate who helped the staff member was released from segregation back to the yard, where he continued his usual activities and returned to his old job in the print shop. Nobody messed with him, but he wasn't shunned for what he did. It was almost business as usual, even though everyone knew what he did. And most staff kept an extra eye on him just in case he was attacked for helping. His parole hearing was moved up about eighteen months, and he was granted an early parole. We were all sure that his actions that day improved his parole chances and may have saved the staff's life. And it reminded us that not all prisoners are bad in all circumstances.

EXCUSES WE'VE HEARD
(AND OTHER FUNNY THINGS)

Here is a compilation of some of the best or funniest excuses we heard.

Remember that inmates have nothing but free time and it made their day to come up with these ideas and use them in their everyday hijinks, but it made also our day to hear them. We always wondered what was coming next.

- That can't be an off-limits area. I don't go in those.
- My bad back was hurting me so much that I couldn't turn left or right; therefore, I had to walk straight into a restricted area.
- The broom and mop weren't working properly, so I couldn't do my job.
- It was so hot in the dorm today that the water in my mop bucket evaporated.
- We weren't fighting. We were shadow boxing, and then he walked into my fists.

- There was a bee on his face, so I slapped it. I didn't want him to get stung.
- We weren't fighting. We were trying out for the wrestling team. (We didn't have one at this prison. Not many prisons do.)
- I didn't steal his jacket. It was cold out, so I borrowed it. I just haven't returned it yet. Besides, it's only been six days.
- My Cellie said his skin was dry and itchy so I was rubbing body lotion on it. (It was 2:35 a.m., both inmates were naked.)
- Don't blame me for your stupidity, Cellie. Take that up with your parents.
- My Cellie said that he had something in his eye. So, I was looking to see if I could see it. That's why we were nose to nose.
- It was so cold in our cell that we had to share blankets because we each had only two, and we had to use our body heat to keep warm. (In the winter, this could almost be true.)
- I forgot to come back to work after lunch.
- I put my shirt in the microwave to dry, but it caught fire.
- I've only been here three days, that's why I got lost. I couldn't find my dorm.
- I left my popcorn in the microwave a little longer because I wanted all the kernels to pop. (Have you ever smelled burnt popcorn?)

- The windows seemed so clean—almost like they had disappeared—that I didn't need to clean them again.
- I fell off my bunk. I slipped in the shower. I got hurt playing ball. (All excuses for, 'I got my ass beat.')
- Remember, there is no crying in prison.

THINGS THAT CONCERNED US

Working in a prison heightens one's senses. Some call it a gut feeling or that sixth sense we all feel occasionally. But when we felt it, we paid attention to it. Hopefully, it would turn out to be nothing, but then again, sometimes it did not. It just made us more aware of our surroundings and the need to keep an extra watchful eye on each other as things were always happening in the yard or in a dorm.

One of the things we didn't say or want to hear was, "It sure is quiet today." Cause that's when the crap usually hits the fan.

One occasion put a major scare into everyone in the institution, where it was heard all the way to the state capitol.

It all started with a rumor that some ammunition was hidden somewhere in the yard—nothing specific, just a rumor. That sent the entire prison into a total and immediate lockdown! These extreme measures are used only when the threat is high. This meant nobody moved in the yard without an escort: kitchen workers, maintenance workers, and medical appointments. If it wasn't an emergency, it could and did wait until later. Cooks, dishwashers, nobody moved.

It was about ten-thirty in the morning when the ammunition was first mentioned. Lunchtime came, so instead of going to the chow hall, it was brown bag time. Usually, two bologna sandwiches, a piece of fruit, maybe a cookie, as well as a boxed drink. That evening, for dinner, each dorm was escorted to the chow hall and back. One wing at a time. Everyone was closely watched to make sure nothing was passed. Shortly after, we were told our shift would be extended until further notice. The second shift was called in early. Special response teams from the surrounding prisons were alerted and called in. Calls were made to the State Capitol, and State Police were mobilized. Metal detectors and probe rods were used to check the yard. We cordoned off and divided the yard into sectors. Each sector was assigned a supervisor and officer. All areas were checked. Weight mats were lifted and checked under. The soft ground, such as sand pits, was scanned with the metal detectors and the probing rods. Nothing was left to chance. Everyone was sent back to their dorm rooms. Cell searches were done. All items were checked. All food items were checked. If it was in a box, it was carefully dumped out and then checked, but we let the inmates put back their own items. Unless in a plastic see-through case, we checked it. Television sets were dismantled, opened, checked, and put back together by maintenance.

All dorms were closed off, meaning nobody was in or out unless it was an emergency, and then they had to be escorted. Nothing was left unchecked. Janitor closets, cubby holes, and any likely hiding places were all searched. A good hiding place was the inside of the shower curtain rods. We checked those, too. Our little handheld mirrors and flashlights got a good workout that day. We looked at, in, and under everything we could. Handheld metal detectors were used on all pillows and mattresses. Nothing was left to chance, this could mean life or death if something was missed. Early on, when this first started, there was a lot of toilet flushing going on, so we knew that a lot of contraband was disposed of, which was okay with us.

The search went on the remainder of the first shift, into the second shift then started into the third shift. We have never seen that many officers or various staff personnel in the yard at one time. Neither had the inmates, based on all the comments we heard. Even the inmates talked among themselves about the number of people around the yard and buildings. The lockdown was called off after the entire yard and dorms were searched. Nothing was ever found, so it was a rumor or the hiding places they used were better than what we could find or knew about.

The person who started the rumor? It turned out he was a snitch of a Lieutenant looking for some special attention, to which he later "confessed" to it being a hoax. After that, anything he told to anyone was taken with a grain of salt. Kind of like that old story of the Boy Who Cried Wolf. Even some of our best snitches said it was a hoax, but we still had to look and check it out. The inmates watched us on this wild goose chase for hours. And they had their chuckles over it. But KARMA has everyone's address, so when we searched their cells, maybe we looked a little too close, or we weren't quite as neat as we could have been. We knew it, as well as the inmates.

Ultimately it was a good training exercise for all of us because it sent a message that WE take our business seriously. We kept our eyes and ears open, always watchful, and listened for the things that didn't seem normal, things that the schemers tried to make look normal so they didn't seem abnormal. If we spotted it, the inmate's trick was to make it seem normal or make some small diversion to get our attention away from what we were checking. Sometimes, things were done just to mess with us and watch our reactions, just to see if we were watching.

When the weather gets bad, with either snowstorms or high winds and tornado warnings, we worry because of the power outages that can come with these storms. Even though the dorms and all buildings are equipped with generators that come on when the electricity goes out, there was usually a pause of two to three seconds before the generator kicked in. That's a long time in total darkness. Close your eyes, and have someone time three seconds for you. See how long that is? A lot can transpire in a dark dorm in those seconds. Someone could 'fall' down the stairs. Chairs, foot lockers, or anything else that is not bolted down, could easily fly from the second floor to the first. With the lights out, of course, nobody sees anything so an inmate might get away with something. Always know your whereabouts and be prepared to move the moment the lights go out to a safe place. Turn your radio volume down so as not to give your position away. Even if it's only a step or two away. I always looked for the nearest open cell, so if needed, I could duck in there and then close the door for protection. If we had to fight, it was better to fight one or two inmates rather than a bunch, so when the lights did come back on, it was important to know who it was by the cell you were in.

There are several things that even made us say…hmmm. Since we are concerned about safety, both ours and theirs, we looked for and were always concerned about weapons of any type, yet we give these to the inmates all the time without thinking about it. Almost anything could become a weapon to a bored and creative inmate. We sell items in the commissary that require can openers. Tuna fish and mackerel soups of all kinds are some of the main items inmates buy. There might be other types of canned goods sold at various prisons. But in order to open those cans that we sell to them, we also have to sell the small handheld can openers. It's not the can opener that's bad, but the end result. The lid of a can, with its sharp, jagged edges, can cause quite a slice. Since it's not a clean-edged cut, it is harder to stitch up when one gets cut, either accidentally or on purpose. It can quickly become a very bloody mess.

Another weapon that we provide is that each dorm has a microwave — not to be used for drying clothes, which was done on more than one occasion. The microwaves were intended to make popcorn, heat water for ramen noodles, a nice cup of hot instant coffee in the morning, in the winter a nice warm cup of cocoa, warm up some soup, or for whatever else needed to be heated up. That is another concern because inmates get creative when they have the time to sit around and think all day. They can heat up water to the boiling point and then use the boiling water as another form of weapon against other inmates as retaliation or as a reminder for whatever grudge or mistake that has happened. Mainly it's used on the inmates as a warning if someone screwed up, got something another inmate wanted or when another inmate got nosey or violated one of the unwritten rules. Mostly, it was warm, really warm, and came with a warning, don't do 'whatever', or else.

Another item that was sold in the inmate commissary was an item called a stinger. It resembles a coil attached to a handle, and as long as it was plugged in, it stayed hot. It was plugged into an electric wall socket, then put in a cup or bowl to keep your coffee hot or make your pinto beans or whatever you want heated up. In the winter, you have a nice hot cup of cocoa while you do other stuff in your cell. Watch TV, read a book clean your area. This seems innocent enough. It got hot enough to boil water, so it got quite hot. The only drawback was that the cord was usually only eighteen inches long, so it could only be used in the cell or a common area close to an electrical socket. These stingers are just about passe now that microwaves are so prevalent.

We've all seen and heard of the prison "cocktails" that inmates concoct and use. It's a mixture of various things. Urine, feces, vomit, spit, toilet water. All mixed together, then thrown at officers through the food slots in the doors or, in the older prisons, the bars of the cell. Very unpleasant and very nauseating, plus the fear of not knowing what diseases the inmates carried. It meant that the staff on the receiving end would become contaminated and have months of extra medical tests and checkups to ensure that they didn't come down with anything contagious. The inmates incurred more charges, but most of them didn't care. It was just another nasty part of the job that we signed up for but didn't want.

Another weird thing that we saw in prison was that some inmates didn't cut their fingernails short. Instead, they let them grow and then filed them to a sharp point and then these could be used as a weapon in the event of a fight to either be used as a sharp slashing weapon or a scratching weapon. You had to get up close and personal to use them, but they were effective. Right after the altercation, the inmate could be cut off, break, or trim their nails and easily discarded them so there would be no evidence. That meant you might get to make your mark without punishment.

There were days that just didn't feel right. If we were working in the dining hall when that feeling came, or all of a sudden, the noisy din of the chow became quiet, there could be a problem. Dead silence. That's the sound we didn't want to hear. The heightened sense kicked in, and then you knew it was time to pay better attention because you knew it would happen inside or outside the chow hall somewhere. Just be prepared and watch the hands and eyes. Two dead giveaways.

THE DIRTY STAFF

Not all staff members were dirty, and mostly, we didn't know who was. We heard inmates talk, but most of the time, the inmates were just speculating or sometimes just trying to get staff in trouble by putting them under suspicion, thereby giving the inmates more time to do their dastardly deeds with fewer people watching. After all, if staff are being looked at, the inmates are left alone. When the staff member did get caught, we were as surprised as anyone else, and then we wondered how long this could have been going on. What was it that was being brought in? Who was their contact inside and outside of the prison? Some questions never get answers. But we kept on listening, especially after a bust. That's when more tongues wagged.

One of the things we always thought of in the back of our minds was, who are the "dirty cops" we had in uniform? The dirty ones saw it as a way to make a few dollars, maybe make friends with the inmates for whatever reason. The money couldn't have been that good. We saw it as a security risk because it made us wonder, "Who can we trust?"

Some kitchen staff workers would occasionally bring in their own lunch for themselves and the other kitchen staff, excluding inmates, of course, on Sunday mornings. It was usually four to five o'clock in the morning and that food was kept warm in the kitchen until it was time for their lunch break or reheated. After all, it was the kitchen. The kitchen staff took turns about who was next and what would be on their menu next. There was one female employee who volunteered to do one Sunday. When that Sunday arrived, she had a case of hamburgers from a fast-food establishment. After going through security at the front desk, the case was opened and just glanced at. Nothing unusual was seen, so nothing was checked underneath the burgers because the front desk officer didn't want to make a mess handling the food. She proceeded as normal towards the walkway after going through two more sally-ports and electronically controlled doors. Now, it was just a short walk to the kitchen. After exiting the building through the sally-ports, she proceeded down the walkway towards the kitchen. The door reopened again, and she was called to by the Internal Affairs Captain; she was then escorted back to the Captain's office, where the local police were waiting. The case of burgers was re-checked by Internal Affairs and the local police. This time, the security officer looked under the food. Inside the burger box, among the onions and pickles, were found several small baggies containing some green, leafy-looking substance, which, when tested, turned out to be marijuana.

During the investigation, as well as subsequent questioning, she revealed it was indeed marijuana. She also stated that once in the kitchen, she would hide the baggies in the food storage room in a pre-designated place. Then, the designated kitchen inmate janitor would pick it up and deliver it to whom it was supposed to go. We could only guess that he wasn't getting his cut of stuff or he wanted a raise, so he ratted out the staff member as to who it was and when the next delivery would be.

That inmate swore to the person who was supposed to get the delivery that he didn't know what happened or how she got busted. The investigation continued after she was escorted out, but it was determined that this had been going on for some time. She never gave up her contact(s) on the yard.

No other inmates were implicated. She was then escorted to TAD, where she was placed in an orange jumpsuit, handcuffed, and walked up the walkway past three dorms that had a clear view of the walkway out to a waiting police car. All this was done in a conspicuous manner so that all the inmates AND staff could observe THIS WALK OF SHAME! As the dirty staff walked out, there was loud cheering going on from the inmates. As she was escorted up the walkway and out the doors to the waiting local police, the worst part was it left the kitchen workers short one person just prior to feeding time because this caused a kitchen staff hardship and shortage. Then, the security officers usually had to supplement the kitchen staff by assisting in the chow hall, creating a shortage in the yard or in the dorm where the officer was taken from. But it sure beats what was going to happen to her. A future not so bright. Maybe even a time coming up on the inside. But not where she was just escorted from.

There was another staff officer who thought she was all IT. She had been working there for about three years and thought she was above everybody else. She didn't talk much, not even to other staff or those who worked with her. She was programmed to work the honor dorm all five days of her work week as this was one of the easier posts to work. The inmates were quieter because some had more to lose, as most had day jobs, so it was noted that the honor dorm inmates were quieter and in bed earlier than the other dorms. But they were also shrewder in what things were done. Their jobs were usually the better ones in the yard. Both in pay and stature among the inmates.

She was bringing in marijuana on occasion. No one ever found out how she got it into the prison or past security, but she was also dating a Lieutenant on the same shift. They usually came in at the same time. Maybe it helped because the Lieutenant was seldom searched as they reported to work together. Talk about a conflict of interest. One crossword to her or about her, she went straight to her boyfriend, and you got the crap assignment for the rest of the shift. She thought she was protected by him or from the front office because of her flirtatious manner to those she thought could help her. It was found out that she was supposed to bring in a substantial amount of marijuana. Internal affairs found out through a snitch in the yard. The State Police were notified of when and where the drop was to take place. A sting was set up, and those involved got their just rewards; again, all this was thanks to a disgruntled inmate who was wronged.

The drop was to occur at a rest stop along an interstate leading to the prison. It was early in the morning when the drop-off and pick-up were planned for. According to the plans, things were going smoothly. The state police in unmarked cars were there for the drop-off when the staff member was there to pick-up. Once the transaction was concluded and filmed, internal affairs and the State Police lit up the parking lot like a tree on Christmas morning in their unmarked cars. Then, it was a downhill ride for them. Only not a joyous one. Word got back to prison that we would be one officer short for that day as well as several more thereafter. The front office wanted to know why no one "up front" was notified of what was happening. The fewer people that knew, the better. Again, loose lips... It couldn't be proven that anyone from the front office had anything to do with it, but... she was terminated, of course. Since nothing could be proven about the boyfriend, he was just transferred to another prison. Nothing could ever be found out about the delivery person either. She went to court, and her case was adjudicated to a lesser charge and settled. We never heard the outcome of her case, and her name was never found in the state prison archives. The front office help that was suspected were exonerated and cannot be revealed for security reasons.

There was even a case of sex for money. Yes, it does happen. The female officer had set up a post office box where the inmate had friends send money orders to it. When she picked up the money, the staff member would contact the inmate, and the rendezvous would be arranged. After all, it was easy for her to arrange for you to be assigned to the right post. As always, the only way for two people to keep a secret is if one of them is dead. But word got out because the inmate would tell his cellmate, who was told to not tell anyone, to which he said, of course not. But his Cellie would just kind of mention it to his best friend, who was told not to tell anyone (of course not) etc., etc. It was another act of jealousy because one inmate had or was getting something the others didn't have but wanted in on it. Soon, word got back to the front office and Internal Affairs. There are no secrets in prison. It just takes a while for them all to get out. So then... another one bites the dust. The staff was fired, and the inmate was transferred out of state. Another tough explanation for the inmate to his family and the staff member to theirs.

These kinds of instances resulted from the inmates talking smack to the staff, listening, and "grooming." It usually happened with the weaker staff who seemed lonely or vulnerable, or even from just talking in general with the inmates, who were listening as if they really cared and paying attention to who was saying what. Hearing things that were wanted or needed could set things into motion. Then, being on the weaker side or caught at a bad time at work, the weaker ones succumbed to the inmates' games of 'love' or the phrase "I know how you feel," showing that these manipulators are all caring and interested in them as a person. The inmate pretended to be helping them to get through their problems as well as the rough times at home or work because they've been there too. All the inmates can and do listen well because it's what they do with all the excess time on their hands. These con men will tell you what you want to hear when you want or need to hear it. They can tell when you are not on your game. It gives them an edge. Your tells that you give off alert the other inmates and by them watching you, you also give yourself away. They can and do watch and listen to slowly groom a person for a long time because they have all the time in the world.

Another kitchen staff member "fell in love" with an inmate due to serve out his sentence in less than six months. That staff and the inmate had an ongoing "relationship" from working in the kitchen together for a long time. So, when the inmates went back to the dorms for the count, on occasion, one or two could be kept back if there was additional work that needed to be done under the supervision of a staff member. How convenient for those two. These two always seemed to end up working the same shift with the same days off. (Over a year long). After hours, the phone calls were frequent. Very frequent. But I guess the inmate and staff forgot to read the signs above all phones that all phone calls are subject to monitoring and recording. Actually, all calls are recorded but only become of interest if need be. After Internal Affairs listened to some of the calls, the Shift Captain called her into the Internal Affairs office. Her husband, who was an officer but in security, was also called into the office. She was asked by Internal Affairs if she was involved with or having an affair with any inmate. After many loud denials, raised voices, and accusations, Internal Affairs said, "Let's listen to this." Internal affairs then played back some of the recorded phone calls, with everyone involved present.

Oops, red-face time. Tears, more accusations from the husband, questions by Internal Affairs, threats by and to both. She finally admitted it was true and what their future plans were. Hell, it was all on tape anyway. She was fired immediately; the inmate was transferred that day; his phone privileges were suspended for a period of time. But they could get another inmate to make calls on their behalf and relay any information, as well as mail coming and going with different inmates' info. The marriage was now done for. The husband then voluntarily transferred to another prison, where he hoped that the news didn't follow him. But the corrections community, as well as the inmates' families, are small, so news, good or bad, travels fast as well as far. He wished her well with a few choice words as she was escorted out the door.

45

As implied before, loose lips sink ships, careers, and marriages. But not all staff personnel are bad or corrupt. Most do a great job without getting caught up in the games inmates play. There is always that one who spoils it for everyone and gives everyone a black eye. I guess it's guilt by association until we earn our honor and respect, which can take a long time.

The bottom line is that it can usually be the result of jealousy. Someone has something that everybody else wants, be it real or suspected. It's all about perception. If that can't happen, then just keep talking. It's a natural urge to talk. In prison, as in most other places, the office, sports games, one tells two, who tells two more, who tells two more now it's eight, and so on. Pretty soon, it's too large to stop. Usually, the entire yard knows what's happening in a very short span of time.

The unfortunate thing is that when dirty staff gets caught if they're convicted and sent to prison, it's usually an out-of-state facility for safety and security reasons. This creates a hardship for their families after you try to explain what happened and why. The visits then become more infrequent as another family is destroyed.

We had another officer who was always jealous of his wife and wanted to keep up with her comings and goings. When he called her, he wanted to know where she was at all times. He would try to smuggle in his cell phone and call at different times just to check on her. But he could never be sure. If he got caught bringing in his phone, the excuse was, 'Oops, I forgot I had it on me,' then he took it back to his car. If he couldn't bring it in, he would call when he went on break, lunch, or dinner.

We had a shift Captain who liked to keep things quiet during his shift. (Hell, we all wanted quiet shifts.) He visited segregation on his shift as required, once a day on the second shift, where we talked about a particular inmate who was always a troublemaker. Generally, they just wanted to smoke a cigarette when tobacco was still allowed in prison.

The Captain instructed me to take the inmate out to the walkway after the mid-shift count to let him smoke a cigarette. I told the Captain that I don't smoke, so I didn't have any cigarettes. He gave me one of his along with some matches. I told the Captain NO, I wasn't going to do this, so we had a few words about it. I eventually told him I would as soon as I did an occurrence report (an internal document that went to Internal Affairs and the Warden). I wasn't a rat, but I also didn't know if this was a test or who was watching me.

The Captian tried to tell me I shouldn't do that (the paperwork), so after much discussion and maybe a slight argument, he finally relented and said, "OK, forget about it." Maybe he got someone on the third shift to do it, but I didn't do it on my shift.

After that, the Captain and I never got along well. We butted heads a few times after that. And, of course, he always won. (Another reason I never got promoted?)

But I can't say that he was dirty. He just wanted to keep the peace and quiet on his shift, even if it meant that he wanted me or somebody else to break the rules.

WHAT'S COOKING IN
THE KITCHEN

All meals were prepared and served by the inmates, who had some general knowledge of how a kitchen operates. They knew their way around a kitchen and its equipment or showed a desire to learn, all under the supervision of qualified staff. Also, they had to learn to remain within the budgetary constraints mandated by the state.

The Food Service Director kept an eye on the budget, but he and his staff mostly fed quality meals to the prison population for about one dollar and change for each person. Herbs and spices were used in all dishes. (Note; we'll come back to this later). Back in the day, the kitchen was under the control of the state. Still, one staff member and one inmate liked experimenting with different ways to prepare and adjust the menu. They concocted an OUTSTANDING pimento cheese spread that everyone raved about, and it was better than any store-bought brand. This was usually served on Fridays, along with a vegetable soup from the leftover vegetables served during the week. Not much went to waste. On holidays like July Fourth, there were hamburgers, hot dogs, corn on the cob, and the usual cookout fare, usually with watermelon for dessert. This was a great treat that the inmates liked. On the big holidays like Thanksgiving and Christmas, there was turkey and ham with all the usual trimmings. It was all prepared by the inmates under kitchen staff supervision. There were even precautions taken for those who had special dietary concerns, IE, no pork or pork products, if there were any allergies, etc. Even during the month of Ramadan, the Muslim population was given special meals and special eating times. Since they didn't eat until after sundown, they used the prison staff dining room.

The kitchen had some great inmate cooks who took pride in what they served even while following the state-mandated menu. There was even an inmate cooking school, taught by certified instructors who gave lessons to inmates who wanted to learn the culinary arts. They even baked some of their own breads or pastries on occasion. The classes usually had six inmates, and they cooked meals every day except on weekends when they were fed by the regular staff and inmates. These were then served to inmates locked up in KCPC and their officer's staff personnel. The classes usually lasted 6 months, and if you were dropped, you could not reenroll. More stringent precautions were taken, and tighter control was in place for all knives used in these classes, even though they were secured to the tables while the class was in session. But all the knives were secured and signed out by staff for use in the kitchen.

These classes also ended when the state ended running the kitchens, which were later contracted out to a private company. The quality of the dining went downhill. Not only did the inmates notice, but so did the staff. The kitchen had to prepare meals for everyone. The prison had a population of around nine hundred fifty, so they had to prepare for that many plus staff members. When the private company took over the kitchen, sales at the inmate commissary went up almost twenty-five percent. This was due to the meals being bland, with no spices or very little seasoning; all meat products were turkey or a combination of turkey or chicken. Even the vegetables were of poor quality. There are typically a few in any situation, such as military mess halls or college dining areas, where not everyone is happy with the food. After all, it's not mama's home cooking. The headcount of inmates eating in the dining hall dropped to around three hundred per meal, which created A LOT of waste for the kitchen. Those who did eat there usually were the ones with little or no money in their book accounts. A lot more mackerel, spam, and ramen noodles were being sold, along with more junk food, like sweets, popcorn, chips, and cookies.

Some even say they stayed away from the dining hall as a protest, but nothing could be done about it. When the kitchen saw how much food was being thrown away, they cut back on how much they prepared. Then everyone showed up to eat, and the kitchen had to scramble to fix more food. They usually kept a back-stock of bologna, ham, and cheese on hand in emergencies.

Of course, the inmates working in the kitchen routinely kept the inmate population informed. The meal cost per person dropped below the one-dollar mark per inmate because inexpensive meals were served with no or little seasonings. Fresh vegetables reappearing and salt and pepper being added were two of the biggest changes.

This little protest lasted for several months until the kitchen company figured out why, and then they changed their ways of doing things. Who says a peaceful, unspoken protest can't change things? They talked amongst themselves and planned things out quietly and orderly when they had to. Inmates aren't all dumb.

The staff dining room was located in the kitchen. It was run by the kitchen staff and inmate kitchen workers. All staff members had to go through the line with their trays served by the inmate working that line. They were given orders by the kitchen supervisor that nobody got larger portions or seconds. So, when staff ate there, they ate the same things with the same amount as the inmates. When the food service was switched to the contract company, the quality went downhill, and many staff quit eating there too. It was brown bag time.

Every cell and the common areas of the dorm are also kitchens for the inmates. After hours, when the kitchen is closed, it's late night, everyone is watching TV, or doing what they do—the hungries get you, you need something to eat. You don't want the usual boring popcorn or potato chips. So, it's time to get creative. Ramen noodles, Mack jack, tuna, or whatever is on hand. Get out the onion's peppers, salt and pepper, hot sauce, or whatever spices you have, and it's time to make a meal. Most inmates can whip up a great meal from almost nothing; they can be quite creative and tasty. There are even some prison recipe books out there written by inmates. You'd be surprised by what's in them; though they may sound gross, they are good. Remember, necessity is the mother of invention.

As an example, this recipe was really popular:
Easy, inexpensive also quite tasty so they say.

Prison Pad Thai

Since rice noodles are not readily available in the inmate commissary, they use what is available. Ramen noodles. It may not have that signature spicy-nutty taste, but it's tasty in its own unique way.

Ingredients:

One package of ramen noodles
Crushed peanuts. Buy them at the commissary and crush them.
Peanut butter
Hot sauce.

How to make it:

Prepare the noodles according to directions and drain off the water.
Stir in the peanuts and peanut butter with the hot sauce.
Top with extra peanuts.

Enjoy.

(All amounts used other than the noodles are at your discretion and taste preferences.)

The walking taco was another favorite that was relatively easy to make. Canned chili is warmed and then poured over or into a bag of corn chips. For a variation of this, they used

Doritos for a cheesier taste. That way, they could munch, walk the yard, or watch a ball game sitting in the bleachers, catching some rays and working on their tans.

Here's an easy one called bag lunch.

Take any food item you have, such as ramen noodles, meat snacks, chili, seasonings, etc.

Combine all ingredients in a plastic bag.

Soak the bag in hot water, or use your stinger or microwave to cook it in boiling water.

Enjoy.

The recipes are endless. They'll invent their own using a trial-and-error method or get help from the other inmates. Occasionally, they'll combine foodstuffs and then share them when they're done. A lot of these recipes call for ramen noodles, a prison staple that's not that expensive, just like back in the college dorm.

One of the best liked and most eaten desserts was the no-bake cheesecake. Take turns buying it, making it, sharing it.

GUARDING THE TOWERS

If an officer wasn't feeling good when it was time to report to work, they could ask the shift supervisor for a lighter post, such as a tower, or the recreation field, relief posts where you give relief to post that need it. Or another where there wasn't much walking or physical activity. After all, we get sick too, so the supervisors knew that we could have called in sick and he would be one person shorter.

Some of the staff officers preferred to work in the towers for various reasons. The shift supervisor usually accommodated them because it was a warm body in a position that needed to be filled. Some of the staff had their own reason for wanting a tower post. They were scared of themselves being in close contact with inmates, and those officers usually didn't last long because you can't do a career in the tower. Fear was usually being scared or unsure of themselves or what to do or not to do. Nobody could know for sure. However, the weaker ones usually leave within six months of being hired. There were officers who liked it because they had an agenda of their own. One liked to take her knitting with her to the top of the tower, where she had seven and a half hours of uninterrupted time to knit things for her kids' and grandkids' personal needs. Slippers, sweaters, mittens, winter hats, and beanies.

Another liked to work the tower on weekends. He liked to eat a lot and grill. So, when he worked the tower, he carried a small hibachi grill with him, along with a good steak and all the fixings to go along with it: baked potato, salad, and a vegetable. All posts, including the towers and dorms, were equipped with microwaves and small refrigerators. Almost all the comforts of home, without a bed. So, he could skip his break, stay in the tower, eat nice, in peace and quiet.

Another permanent tower guard was someone who was finally close to retirement. He had slightly less than one year left to go. He was a whiz at computer tech support and repairing computers, so when he was in his tower, he brought his computer repair shop with him to work, repairing computers while passing time in the tower.

The captain's office knew of all these goings on, but these were posts that needed to be filled so what these officers did was provide a warm body to fill that spot. No one ever tried to escape, the prison was secure. All of these were on the second shift. I don't know what took place on the third shift as I seldom worked these shifts.

SELF PRESERVATION

THEIRS...

All officers had things to do every day besides "just" watching the inmates. Some inmates had to be escorted to different areas. Some had to work the chow hall when it was feeding time. Pill Call line. Inmate commissary line. Taking inmates to Transportation to be processed out or in. Outside doctor's appointments. Helped out in the various ongoing classes. Oversee the law library or school classes. So, there was forever something taking officers away from the regular posts, which gave the inmates more time to scheme and plan their next adventure.

Being locked up in prison doesn't mean that all your problems go away. The eyes and ears that were outside extend to the inside. Phone calls, newspapers, and computers are everywhere. So, problems are easy to follow you around. If you ratted on someone out there in court, it could follow you inside. Vengeance and retaliation are never far away.

One way that those who fear for themselves react is with self-protection. That can mean taking magazines, tape several together, and then wrapping them around your body under your clothes. This forms a type of "body armor" to stop prison shanks and shivs should someone try to use one on you. So now that you know who is after you, you can take more precautions to evaluate the threat against you.

While in your dorm or room, you are a little more protected. This is your safe haven. A lot of the rooms have a sock with small pieces or a bar of soap in it. Ask what they are for, and you will be told that it's an air freshener, which could be because it does smell like one. It's also close at hand, always ready at a moment's notice if needed as a weapon. Just like a lock in a sock or a can in the hand. Small, portable, easily disposed of.

Someone who is really scared can even buy protection. All that is required is to pay the protection fee, which is a set amount agreed upon. The money is sent into the protector's account or books from your family. You can also always use the inmate canteen to buy groceries, stamps, etc. But this puts another burden on your family, put there by your poor past actions. Hopefully, maybe the protection can ease up somewhere down the line. But a "contract" may be hard to cancel so be careful before engaging in one. It's either pay or don't get involved; that's a wise choice. Joining a gang isn't that much of a help either because once in, you're in, and when the stuff hits the fan, you have to get involved. No matter what.

Keep yourself hydrated and eat healthy. Don't rely on the canteen food or snacks that you have to buy for your major food intake. The prison food may not be the best but it's healthier than all that junk food. It's also free. So, unless you have unlimited funds learn how to stretch your money. Bulk up with exercise and weights. The bulkier you are the more likely you'll be left alone.

Depression hits everyone. Don't be afraid to talk to your CTO or tell him or her what's going on. The CTOs can refer you to the right person or make appointments for you.

Try not to get angry. The other inmates may take it wrong; they may not know what's going on with you. Don't look for a fight, but don't run from one, either. It shows weakness. Be prepared to fight. Defend yourself only if or when you have to, or you'll be labeled a "punk," then it only gets worse from there. You may lose a fight or two, but you have proved a point that you are nobody's 'punk,' and you're more likely to be left alone.

Never fight until you have to. But when it is time to fight, fight like you're the third monkey on the ramp to Noah's ark, and it's beginning to rain!

...AND OURS

When someone gets hired in the DOC, they never know what to expect. Some may have prior experience as police, either in the military or civilian world. Or they transfer from the local county jail to the state or federal prison system. Although somewhat similar, they are quite different.

The inmates are like us in some ways. Everyone is resistant to change. The prison system is also new to us, and like them, we have to adjust to this new environment, learning the new ways, ours and theirs. Some new officers come into the prison with their badges on their chests, thinking, "Ok. There's a new sheriff in town," without learning or getting used to their new environment. The inmates are looking for officers who are firm, fair, and consistent. If you work in the dorms a lot, it becomes "your house." If you come to work every day and act the same way every day, you generally won't have any problems with inmates no matter where you work. Remember, they are constantly watching and observing everything you do.

The inmates talk among themselves, so if you're good, they'll pass it along. If you act like you're the boss, or it comes across as 'I'm the one with the badge' or 'because I said so, you will do as I say when I say,' there will be problems. Inmates know the drill of what happens, and when it's supposed to happen, so they can slowly walk you, taking their time doing things to generally make your life slow and miserable. After all, they want consistency, too.

If you tell an inmate you're going to do something, like get some information on a program or something special that is going to happen, or what's going on the next day in the gym or rec field or whatever, follow up and do it. Don't make stuff up. If you don't know, don't lie or bullshit them because they'll find out, and there goes your credibility. They may not like the answer you provide, but at least you got them an answer. Surprisingly, they'll help you keep your house straight. If you make a mistake, hell, apologize. After all, you're only human too. They will respect that.

Inmates can be 'friends 'with the officers without crossing any boundaries. They talk with the officers, shoot the breeze, and somewhat assist the officers in their job by doing their (the inmate's) jobs a little better, cleaner, or tidier. Inmates may even tell officers their problems just to have someone to talk to other than a CTO or their cellmate. Some inmates even see the officers as father or mother figures because they didn't have one at home, so they might be looking for a little guidance. Sometimes, they unknowingly snitch someone out without realizing it. It's usually the inmates who snitch on the dirty staff.

Convicts, on the other hand, only talk to the 'screws' or turn keys when they have to. Then, they usually have another inmate with them and talk a little louder so others can also hear that they are not ratting out someone. A convict is someone who goes to prison and just doesn't want to conform. They want to be left alone to do their time. They don't try to make your life miserable, but they won't make it any easier, either. They still resent you and all you stand for. (Like the establishment.)

Old school convicts make up only about twenty percent of any institution, so it's getting less in today's era of me-first-and-only type of inmate. They will also snitch on dirty staff if it's to their advantage. But it's always good to remember that the officer is outnumbered, sometimes as in a full dorm by one hundred eighty inmates to one or two officers on the floor at any given time. So, if the officer wants to be badass, go ahead and try the inmates. See what happens when the lights go out. Cause yours might!

The officer can be hard and straight at the same time. Just be like that every day. Or, you can be like, 'I'm looking to put pen on paper or write you up. To make your life miserable as hell because you're a convict, or I'm the one with the badge.' You also need to learn which of the rules you can bend, break, or ignore.

As I stated before. Being Firm, Fair, and Consistent goes a long way.

But NEVER mistake an officer's kindness for weakness.

There are many more instances like this, but I'm sure you get the point.

SOLITARY LIFE

Life in solitary is certainly not easy. The typical cell that we had was approximately seven feet wide by eleven feet deep. Most bathrooms in homes are bigger than this. In this cell was a metal bed that was bolted to the floor. A stainless steel sink was attached to a stainless steel toilet, which was attached to the wall and floor. The distance from your dining table to your toilet was about four feet. Imagine if you can, a stainless-steel toilet in the middle of winter. The cells were 'comfortable' but not overly warm. Your butt heat would warm it up in a few minutes, so it was a comfortable temperature. Also in the cell was a stainless-steel table about eighteen inches square with a round seat that was comfortable for about the first twenty minutes unless you used your pillow as a cushion. Then, it was time to move around and rest up your derriere. That was your writing table, your dining table occasionally as a stool when you needed a change of furniture. Add your mattress, pillow, and some bedding. That's it. A few books, add any legal papers that you want, and call it home.

So, you walk it. Count the steps from the cell door to the far wall. Then, side to side. Then, around the entire room. Mark it down. Then, keep track of how many times it takes to walk around the entire room to make a mile. Then, figure out your mileage. It helps to keep the mind occupied and a record of your personal goals. If your stride is eighteen or twenty-four inches... there's your math problem for today. Remember, it takes five thousand two hundred eighty feet to make a mile, so how many miles do you walk in a day, or how many miles did you make for your entire stay in segregation?

Run or jog in place. Do sit ups. Pushups. Do some jumping jacks. Put your books or legal papers in a pillow case lift some weights. Whatever it takes to stay in shape if you are so inclined to do. It helps to pass time and keeps your mind off other things.

Time in solitary, to some, is just a short respite from the mundane life that you lead in the yard for a few days or weeks. It can be a hiding place to escape if needed for a variety of reasons. Sometimes, inmates, especially the newer ones or weaker ones, get scared being in the yard, so they approach an officer and request to "check in" to get off the yard. When this happens, for whatever reason, they "check in" (say it fast), and it gets translated to chicken or PC," prison chicken" in prison terms. But its true meaning is Protective Custody. There are plenty of ways to get to solitary for short periods of time. Find an officer or supervisor request to check in, or give some bogus reason that'll get you off the yard for a few days while you re-group to get your shit together. Or you can start an altercation with another inmate but don't get too physical because now you've made an enemy for later. Or just say that you are planning to get someone for whatever reason until that can be investigated just enough to get off the yard; that's usually good for a week, but then it's back to the yard.

Some inmates who are CIs (Confidential Informants) get found or if just suspected of being one, are warned to get off the yard or else. If that's the case, transfer is usually not far behind. Either to another facility within the state, an interstate compact, or a transfer to another state for more security, depending on what your crime was. But remember that the mail and phone calls go both ways, so whatever usually catches up with you no matter where you go.

Some go to the hole to settle debts or to collect a debt. If someone owes a debt and is in solitary, what better way to get visited by the debt collector? So, if you're in the wrong wing, just tell the case worker that you have a conflict with someone in that wing and get moved. But debts in prison never go away. Your debts will follow you around until they get paid off. All debts can be sold, bought, or traded to someone else. The best thing is to avoid going into debt. Paybacks are a bitch. But some inmates just need time to get their act together.

An existence in the hole can be exhausting on the body as well as the mind, especially for those who are already not mentally or physically strong. Long stretches in solitary can exasperate it even more. For those of us who had daily contact with those in solitary for long stretches, we could notice the subtle changes in their mental status.

We noted these changes or any other changes in the daily logs that we had to keep on each individual. This was along with noting if all meals being eaten. Is the inmate changing clothes on a regular basis, taking their meds, showering regularly, did they participate in recreation? All of the small mundane things that we were required to monitor each day, by each shift.

There was one inmate who checked into segregation every year just about the same time. The same month, same day. He would then go on a hunger strike. He refused all nourishment each meal. Fruits, sweets, eggs, cereal. After several days, he refused almost all liquids. Milk, coffee, juice. He only took water and very little of that. So, he knew what he was doing. On shower nights, he even refused that. He did not go out for recreation; he just lay on his mattress or sat at his tiny bedside table. Just sat and stared at…nothing. The psychologist, case worker, and the warden all talked to him to no avail. I knew him from when I worked in the dorms, and I tried talking to him. Nothing.

For sanitary reasons, the warden ordered him to be given a shower. He was placed in the restraint chair and wheeled into the shower, where we proceeded according to the wardens' instructions. We didn't scrub him. We just let the water cascade down on him. He was then returned to his cell, where he just laid on his bed. He was then placed in an observation cell under twenty-four-hour watch. There, he remained for a total of 18 days, with nothing to eat and just a few sips of water. We could see his weight go down as his health declined.

When he returned to "normal," he asked for food. So, we checked with medical as to how to proceed. He was slowly given what was needed to build back his strength and get back some muscle tone and mass. I had the opportunity to talk with him several weeks later when I asked him what was up with his behavior. He told me that it was in remembrance of his brother, who died in prison several years earlier. That was the end of the conversation, and neither of us mentioned it again. He completed his sentence several months later and then was released on parole. He was always a quiet guy; he just minded his own business. Someone who wanted to be left alone.

A way for the inmates to stay in contact with each other was to pass along information while trying not to arouse suspicion, this was called fishing. The inmates would take notes, secure them with a piece of string, usually taken from their uniforms or bed sheets, and secure the string to the notes or kites. Keep sending it down the walkway until it gets to the right person. The next person would tell someone across the hall or walkway to pass it along to the cell next door or across the hall, and then finally, to the intended recipient. The buddy system worked well because as it was being passed along, no one had time to read it. Besides, everyone was being watched on that walk. Sometimes, we would see this, and we would try to intercept the mail, but when the electronic door opened, the telltale sound of a loud click was heard, and the 'kite' was either quickly hidden or flushed. If it hadn't been flushed, it could have been put in with their legal papers because that was a safe place.

Another trick they used was to tie a piece of string to the contraband flush it after it had been wrapped in cellophane paper that we provided them with some of their lunches. It would only go as far as the string was long. If we found something, the first thing they usually said was, "it's not mine. Did you do a clean cell search before I moved in here"?

How do you survive the solitary life? Here are a few hints. Develop a routine and try to maintain a daily schedule. Remember what you did, what you used to do, when, where, and how. Write it down, go over it. Add to it. Revise it. Keep the mind occupied. Build a house in your mind, remake it, draw it, redesign it, then draw the plans for it. Whatever you choose to do, you have to keep your mind busy.

When living in the dorms, all inmates can have a small cooler that is used as a refrigerator, kept cool from the ice machine in each dorm. It can be a hassle, but it keeps the inmate's perishables from going bad. It also provides ice if they want a cool drink. Another good hiding place was in the lid of the cooler. They would carefully pry open the lid and remove some of the insulation, and then it became a place to hide small items, such as betting slips or extra pills that they had accumulated. It took a close inspection to see this, as a lot of times, the officer was in too much of a hurry to pay too close attention to detail. Coolers were not permitted in solitary, so everything was usually room temperature except the two plastic cups of juice they received at mealtime.

Another tool that was used in segregation was an item called a suicide vest or smock. It was basically two quilted, somewhat insulated pieces of cloth about as thick as a light blanket. It was sleeveless and hung from the shoulders down to about the mid-calf range. It was held together at the shoulders by two Velcro straps. These suicide vests are used to 'ensure warmth and comfort' while not obstructing the wearer's movements. It also could not be rolled or torn and was rip-resistant, so it couldn't be torn up and used for other purposes, such as tying it together to try to hang oneself. If someone tried to do self-harm, they were put in segregation and all of their personal items, especially clothing, were removed, and they were given this protective smock to wear until the psychiatrist cleared them to have their items returned to them.

LIGHTEN THE MOOD

There were days when things became tense, or things just didn't feel right. Something was off. The inmates could feel it. We could feel it. It was that gut feeling that you sometimes get regardless of the situation. (Don't ignore that gut feeling, it's usually right). There was nothing that caused it or made it stand out. It was just there. Maybe it was the full moon syndrome, a change in the atmosphere or barometric pressure, or just being cooped up. On those days, the end of the shift couldn't come fast enough. So, we had to come up with ways to lighten up the mood and try to diffuse any situation before it got out of hand.

While out on recreation, we could have eleven inmates at one time. Five on one side, six on the other. One side had a basketball goal for a little more fun that we assumed was for their gambling interests. Three on three was a good game they enjoyed, so a good sweat could be worked up when playing hard. Hopefully, it was going to be shower night. If not, it was taking a bath the best they could using just their sink. It usually made a mess on the floor, but that would dry up, evaporate, and help cool things down. Basketball also helped to release tensions. Occasionally, for an added incentive, we would offer a cup of coffee to the winning team or to an individual if he could make the free throws from a particular spot. Or who could make the most out of ten? After all, it was just a cup of coffee, but it helped take the edge off the day. They always tried to finagle more out of us just for the hell of it cause it's the games they played. It developed a little trust between us and the inmates, but we all knew that it was us against them and would always remain so.

There were the occasional fights while out on recreation. Some were just because of escalating arguments, some from the game, or from retaliation for something that happened before. Or just more trash-talking to pass the time of day. After all, what were we gonna do? Lock 'em up in segregation?

One individual was locked up because he said he had thoughts of self-harm. It was a corner cell with a large three-foot by three-foot unbreakable window that we used for observation when needed. He would bang his head on the glass window to get attention. I was working in the control center when he said he would do a head dive off the stool in his cell. It was about three feet off the floor attached to the wall. I notified the supervisor on duty, and he tried to talk to him, but to no avail. The inmate knew we were all watching, and it was being recorded on camera. So, he did his dive, but just before he hit the floor, he extended his arms just enough to break his fall before he did a fake face plant. He laid there for a few moments, then slowly got up, looking like he was hurt or in great pain. I took a piece of paper, got a magic marker, and wrote the number 8.5 on it, just like scoring an event at the Olympics. I showed him the 'score' through the window. We both got a good chuckle out of it. Got to lighten the mood. I told him later, when I was on floor patrol, that I did see his fake dive and how he caught himself. And that he'll never be an Olympic diver.

When in their cells, the inmates talked a lot amongst themselves. In their cells, they tried to speak through the slot where the door opens or the food slot. Being in all concrete "boxes," the cells and hallway sounded like talking into a fifty-five-gallon drum. It echoed. A lot.

There was one inmate who was slightly overweight. He was new to the prison, so he had that bewildered look of 'what's going on here?' as he tried to find his place. He wanted to show himself as being harder than he was. He would go to the gym or the outdoor weight pile daily and go through his weight-lifting regimen. When he returned to the dorm, he was sweating up a storm. I finally asked why, and he said he was trying to lose some weight. I then asked what he was doing that caused him to sweat that much all the time. He lifted his shirt up, and his body was wrapped in trash bags, causing him to sweat excessively and lose water weight. I told him to quit and to unwrap himself because it could cause more significant health problems than help by becoming dehydrated. I also had to periodically and randomly check him to be sure he complied, which he was doing.

The more articulate ones tried to crack us up with their jokes and stories. Most stories were probably made up, so it was their intent to try to get a rise out of us. If the story was told more than once, they became more embellished each time. Trying to make the story more interesting or make themselves look bigger, badder, or better. Stories of what occurred back home on the block, with those who were once their runnin' buddies with all their exploits. Some officers even reciprocated with their own stories. Were they ever embellished? Of course, they were! Everyone was trying to one-up each other. After all, we all love to tell stories and be heard. Always remember that all stories start either of two ways: 'Once upon a time' or 'This ain't no shit.' We all wondered who had the best stories. Every one of these guys sure had some tall tales. But don't we all?

Since all posts are almost identical for all shifts, there are some posts that are just plain boring. These occur during the second or third shift periods when things are slower. It's darker outside, so there is less happening and less movement in the yard or outside in the parking lot. One such post is driving the perimeter road. This post requires you to drive the perimeter in a random pattern because the inmates are always watching for patterns and taking notes. Checking fences for any breaches and doing fence checks to make sure that the fence alarms are in working order. This is done on all three shifts. Suppose you're tired or had a long day before coming to work, and it's a cool or cold evening. In that case, you have the heater in the car going, the radio is playing your favorite tunes, and its easy for the officer on this post to sometimes get drowsy. So, you go to the far side of the perimeter road where it's hard to be seen from any of the towers and that's where you put the car in park. Shut off the lights, but keep the car running and rest just for a moment. Sure, you tell yourself just for a minute… slowly your eyes close… sometimes you doze off or fall asleep. You haven't been seen for a while, so the other towers call you on the radio, trying to get your attention, but if you're sleeping, you hear nothing. After several attempts to contact you, one or two towers notified the Captain's office that they hadn't seen the perimeter vehicle in a while because something may have happened to the driver. On one occasion, the Shift Lieutenant tried to get in contact with the officer but to no avail. So, he got a second vehicle and drove out to see what happened to the first perimeter car.

The Lieutenant spotted the parked car, and he didn't know what was up, so he parked a short way away so he could walk up to the parked perimeter car. He snuck up on it just in case. Well, lo and behold, there was the driver, who was now fast asleep.

The Lieutenant then knocked on the driver's window of the car. He had his pistol out, just in case, so the driver could see it when he woke up. The driver woke up startled and jumped a bit. He knew that he was busted. The Lieutenant then told him to drive the car to the front of the Administration Building. He was relieved of his post, paperwork was done reflecting what happened, and another officer was assigned to that post for the remainder of the shift. The officer caught sleeping was given a letter of reprimand, which was placed in his file. It was a long time before he got that easy perimeter post-assignment again.

Different church softball teams contacted the prison when they wanted to come in, play the inmates in softball or basketball, and talk about religion and being saved. These would have to be scheduled several weeks in advance so things could be set up, background checks run, and things could be accommodated for them to come in. Both the inmates and the church folks enjoyed these sports and religious interludes. The games usually were double-headers. They were multi-faceted when they did happen. First, neither side wanted to lose, so they played hard. Especially the inmates. It was like they had something to prove by saying that they were better.

The games were usually seven innings, so they could get the two games in. They always started with brief introductions, handshakes, and several prayers. After the first game, it was usually close to lunchtime, so all players and guests were escorted to the dining hall to break bread together. They intermingled while eating, the church folks gave the blessing, and the conversation turned to religion and their salvation. Some of the inmates were not interested but listened because it was different on a different day. But there were those who were genuinely interested in hearing what the guests were saying and preaching. These folks then kept in touch with the inmates who wanted to hear, so the inmates could learn more. Then, it was on to game two, with more competitive sportsmanship taking place. Afterward, it was more prayers, handshakes, and hugs, and then it was time for the church folks to depart. Many acquaintances and friendships were made for future times. Some even asked to be baptized in future meetings together. This had to be pre-arranged with the front office with the cooperation of the prison chaplain. When some of the inmates were paroled, they joined the church that came to visit them. However, they could not come back in to visit or play ball with those who were still incarcerated due to security reasons.

These church visits were not limited to softball. Other teams visited and played basketball as well. In the end, it was all about friendship, fellowship, and respect for each other as humans, whether free or not.

In any type of setting where you have a lot of people gathered together, there are going to be many who gravitate together for different purposes. Either it's the same background from where you came from or the interests you all have, whatever they are. Maybe it's sports or music. When it was music, a lot of the inmates came together. They all find out what they played musically and where their interests lay. Soon enough, they were jammin' together, getting their groove on and making music. Then, it was practice, practice, and more practice. As they played together and got good, they even put a program together and played concerts in the yard for the entire population. Not everyone attended the concerts that were put on, but those who did always had a good time just kicking back and enjoying the music. And they played a great variety. Soul, blues, country, rock, and the oldies, and they were good. It was something different for all around to enjoy.

Board games were another favorite activity of the inmates in the dorms, as they helped them pass the time and relieve some boredom. The game CLUE didn't go well because they accused each other of murder in the library with a lead pipe. To most, it was funny. To a few... not so much. (I guess the truth hurts) so, that game didn't get played a lot. A game that a lot of inmates enjoyed was MONOPOLY. They all played to see who gets the most money, and of course, that translated into cold, hard prison money. Can't stop gambling when there are no scorecards. The only problem with this game was two cards were missing. One is from the Community Chest, and the other is from the Chance cards. The two missing cards? GET OUT OF JAIL FREE. Maybe they thought they could really be used.

CELL SEARCHES

Sometimes, as we did our wing patrols, we would hear little snippets of conversations that caught our attention. Upon leaving that walk, we would signal the Control Center officer to listen to a certain cell to see if he could hear any more. Most of the time, it was just idle chatter, but occasionally, it led to some juicy information that led to a productive search of their cell or someone else's. Sometimes, it led to an ongoing investigation into segregation or elsewhere in the yard. The information we got we would pass on to the appropriate investigative team, or just usually Internal Affairs. Some were productive, some not. But everyone should remember that "loose lips sink ships." So, keep on talking. You never know when we are listening.

While the inmates were out on recreation, we had an opportunity to do a more thorough cell search. We checked the few nooks, crannies, small, tight holes, and cracks. We also thumbed through the mail, looking for anything unusual. We did not search their legal papers, as they were off-limits.

We even looked into their shampoo and body lotion bottles. We would hold a flashlight up to the back side of the bottle with the light toward us to see if anything in the bottle would cast a shadow. If we did see one, we emptied the bottle, saving the contents for the inmate to pour back into the original container. There were not a lot of places to hide contraband, with only a bunk, sink, toilet, tray table, and seat in the cell. The air vents were another popular place to try to hide things. A three-inch by twenty-four-inch window that didn't open was their only contact with the outside other than being on recreation.

Everyone who came to segregation was allowed to bring their own bible when they got locked up. A favorite trick was to peel back the front or back cover of the bible, then spread a thin layer of tobacco in, and then reseal the cover. They used the small pocket bibles for the rolling papers because the pages closely mimicked regular rolling papers. The matches and strikers were then put in the book's spine with the matches torn in half, so now it was two instead of one. It was just one of the tricks they used, but we tried to check things well. Usually, we could feel the bump in the cover, and we would find it all. Then, another charge of bringing contraband into segregation was added to their list of charges. Ahh, the games being played. Some played them well, while others did not.

The bolder or more innovative individuals would get whatever they wanted to smuggle, roll it nice and thin, and wrap it in plastic, small and as tight as they could. They would use plastic wrap from the kitchen that once held sandwiches, and then it was time to hide whatever they were trying to hide.

These were then placed in the body cavity, known as a butt plug. Sometimes referred to in prison slang as a 'permanent pocket.' Some even made them each day just in case they went to the hole for something. Prior planning... Yeah, that's got to have a distinctive flavor to it. But if we suspected it or knew of it, we would have them do a squat and cough when we processed them into segregation. This procedure usually had them expel whatever was in the cavity. If they tried to fake it, we had them give us a heartier cough. Although some got through, it was always cat vs mouse.

The caseworker made his rounds daily. If the inmate in segregation had any requests, such as phone calls, medical needs, or commissary items, yes, they were allowed items such as stamps, writing paper, cards, and hygiene items; they had to be ordered through the caseworker; these items were usually delivered on Saturdays. No food items were allowed in segregation besides the kitchen's three meals. For some, it was a blessing. It helped them to lose weight. It was not a great weight loss program, but for some, it worked. The same goes for smokers. Usually, after thirty or sixty days with no tobacco, they were 'cured' until they got out of segregation. Then it was light up as soon as possible. Of course, all tobacco was banned in the prisons several years later for everyone's health, staff as well as inmates. The state even provided smoking cessation classes with free nicotine patches in order to help them quit.

All their mail received was opened and checked, just in case. The unit caseworker screened all incoming legal mail before delivery and opened it in front of the inmate, who had to sign for it.

PILL CALL

Delivering medications in segregation is a three-times-a-day ordeal. Some inmates get medications morning, noon, or night, so medical had to send a nurse to segregation to dispense the meds since we are not trained medical personnel and cannot distribute medication.

Most inmates knew what meds they took, what they looked like, or what the colors were. If the manufacturer changed the shape or color as they sometimes do, the eagle-eyed inmates noticed this and would question it. When the nurse arrived, a pill call was announced for everyone to be up fully dressed with a cup of water in hand. We watched the pill go from the nurse to the inmate to their mouth. Then, we watched as the inmates had to lift their tongues to show that they had swallowed their meds. But sometimes, the hand is quicker than the eye. Some were very good at the art of hiding a pill in their mouth.

One of the favorite tricks was to stick an envelope to the door just below the food slot opening, and as the pills were transferred, the sneaky ones tried to drop some into the envelope for later use for trade or sale. It was usually the pain meds or the psychotropics that were the main pills that were abused.

Some inmates waited for the nurse to come through for pill or sick calls. The sicker or sneaky ones would stand by the door doing their self-gratification "thing" as they engaged the nurse in conversation. This was easy for us or the nurse to observe because their hands were not visible. When this happened, the conversation was over, and so was their pill call or sick call. The nurse then moved on to the next person to receive meds. It didn't happen often, but it did occur. Sometimes, another charge was added to them, but we always asked if it was worth it since we would have to keep them around for a longer period. During pill calls, it was one of the times inmates got to talk to someone other than the usual segregation staff, so they tried to keep the nurse engaged in conversation for as long as they could. Explaining non-existent ailments just to have the nurse hang around a little bit longer for a change of view. After all, they were seeing a female instead of us. Asking about the latest news, sports, or current events. They asked us also because it kept the nurse around a bit longer. Sometimes, it's just everyday BS. The nurses were not too interested but sometimes just listened and talked as they made their rounds. But they were also wise to what the inmates were trying to do.

Occasionally, an inmate would skip their meds because they were sleeping or didn't want to get up. So, when the inmate did get up for the next pill call, they would ask if they could have the pill or pills that they missed at the last pill call. Of course, the answer was always no, and then sometimes the inmate would cuss out the nurse because they didn't get any meds; they say they needed them to survive or to keep their mind mellow.

To quiet them down, the nurse would always say 'you should have been up before,' which sometimes had a tendency to piss them off more. Sometimes, it made them madder and more demanding. For some, it was an excuse to go off. Then, it was fighting time.

CONFLICTS

Conflicts in prison are almost a way of life. After all, with upwards of eight hundred to twelve hundred (or sometimes more) inmates put together in small, enclosed spaces, that's a lot of testosterone in one place, so things are bound to happen. Being in such close proximity, it's easy to get on each other's nerves. After all, contrary to belief, not everyone is one big happy family. When conflicts did happen, it was always best to try to settle them without being seen to keep from going to solitary. Those not involved wisely stayed as far away as possible to keep from being associated with the trouble or possibly catching another charge.

Some of the conflicts were caused by the inmates knowing each other from the street gangs: the Crips, Bloods, and Aryan Nation. Although there are gang factions in every prison, our prison was not as profound as those on the East or West Coast. The gang members usually kept to themselves, but they occasionally co-mingled. This didn't mean they were breaking bread, but sometimes, it was better to go along to get along in these conditions. The gang's rulers divided the yard, and everyone knew where the boundaries were, or they were quickly informed of them. As usually happens when a lot of different cultures and backgrounds get close together, skirmishes are bound to happen. Then, leaders usually took care of these even before the correctional staff knew what had gone down. Most conflicts were checked before the inmates entered prison, but occasionally, some slipped through the cracks during orientation and in-processing.

Sometimes, the conflicts got bad enough and eventually escalated into a major disturbance involving more than two or three people. I've seen the aftermath of someone falling over a second-story railing that surrounded the stairs. Nobody was killed, but it was a bloody mess for the janitors to clean up after taking all the necessary bio-hazard precautions. As usual, nobody saw anything. A crime scene in the prison. Who would've thought it?

Another way conflicts were settled without being observed, was several other inmates would create a diversion in one place, so the actual retaliation was happening elsewhere, such as in a cell, the shower, or just outside the front doors where the cameras had a blind spot. The inmates knew all the places that were not being watched, where they were located, and where to stand so as not to be seen. Later, if any marks were found on an inmate or any cuts or bruises when questioned, the answer was always, "It happened when I was playing basketball or baseball."

Some were settled while out on recreation. Once the inmates were outside and locked in their respective sides, or bullpens as they were referred to, they had approximately one minute before we could respond and get the gates unlocked to separate them.

Recreation would suddenly end, sending they went back to their cells so the investigation could begin. Someone then was moved to another wing until everything was resolved one way or another. These altercations were always short but sometimes not so sweet. A lot of fists can fly in two minutes. Remember, you could run, but there was nowhere to hide. The tower posts could keep an eye on them.

Some officers who worked at the prison grew up in the same city as some inmates, they even went to school together and graduated with some inmates currently doing time. Since some officers knew some of the inmates personally from back in the day but did not have a real closeness now, it didn't become a conflict. The officers knew them from attending school together, playing sports together, having classes together, or running around together if they were friends back in the day. As everyone got older, their lives came to a fork in the road. Some took the right road; some took the wrong road. For some who took the wrong road, they ended up here, behind the fences. Although it could have been a conflict of interest every time someone came in that was known, an occurrence report had to be prepared, and that employee had to be interviewed by Internal Affairs. The main question that was always asked was if the staff member involved could maintain being firm, fair, and consistent. After all, it was either the transfer of a lot of inmates or one staff member. If the staff officer said that they could truly be professional, then they were.

CELL ENTRIES IN SEGREGATION

We had an officer that we called "the bulk." He was about six feet three, close to three hundred pounds. He looked very intimidating when you first saw him. His position was always on the shield. As the first one to enter a room, his job was to pin or secure the inmate to the floor, bed, or wall to immobilize him. The rest of the team was right behind him, doing what they were instructed to do and what we had practiced. The actions of the cell entry team were prearranged before any entry was made. All cell entries were recorded on a video camera. That officer never overdid his job, but he also gave no quarter. Sometimes, just his size was enough to stop a lot of stuff. But in case the stubborn ones didn't want to comply, we always asked first by showing them the stun shield in action. Just a brief press of the button showed them exactly what fifty thousand volts sounded like and what it looked like, along with a few sparks of electricity. A nice loud ZZZZZAPPING sound was sometimes all it took for some individuals. Some complied; some didn't. Tsk-Tsk. Seven looooong seconds. Oops. Their mistake. Once activated, it cannot be turned off until it runs its seven-second cycle, or the stun shield is removed from the person.

Whenever we had to do a cell entry, we had a game plan: who was in what position, who was on the stun shield, who was on the camera. (This was usually a segregation staff member). After all, we didn't want anyone to get hurt, the inmate or us. After it was over, when things calmed down a bit, everyone involved had paperwork to do, which had to accompany the video to the Internal Affairs office for review by IA, the Shift Captain, the Deputy Wardens, and the Warden.

The inmate was usually just pissed at something or someone or just plain bored. It caused some excitement and broke up the monotony of the day. While we or the psychologist tried to talk them down, sometimes that didn't work, so we had to go in. This was everyone's last resort. Most cell entries were over in a matter of minutes... but there were a few that were worse... but one was particularly disgusting.

There was one individual who took his glasses and broke them in pieces. He took the arms of the frames, sharpened them on the floor of his cell, and then proceeded to cut himself as much as he could with the small pieces of metal or plastic. Inmates always did it the wrong way. They tried to cut going across from left to right instead of going up the arm. Guess they really weren't trying too hard. Nothing was too deep or drastic enough to cause major physical harm. It caused a lot of blood, which made it look much worse than it was, sort of like the death of a thousand cuts. Not one cut was deadly enough to kill, but altogether, it could cause major trauma and create quite a hell of a mess.

One of the supervisors we had in segregation was doing a patrol when he noticed a cell with the window in the door covered. The Lieutenant knocked on the door and told the inmate to remove the cover. There was no answer, so the Lieutenant knocked again and told the inmate to remove the covering. Again, nothing. A third try, but still nothing. The Lieutenant then told me to open the door.

This was a mistake on both our parts because he couldn't see what was going on in the cell since the window was covered. I opened the door, and the inmate came running out, buck naked, covered in blood, feces, lotion, and shampoo, making himself very slippery. He ran to the end of the walk, turned around, and ran back again. He grabbed the Lieutenant, and it was on. The Lieutenant and the inmate started to wrestle and ended up on the floor. I called for backup, and when the backup officers arrived, it was over in a matter of minutes. The Lieutenant was checked by medical, and then he went home early to shower and change his clothes. The inmate showered and was seen by medical for his cuts. Although he had no major injuries, he had to be tended to. After some alcohol wipes and much hollering and yelling, he was returned back to his cell. While this was all happening, the rest of the inmates on that walk were all whooping and hollering because the inmates thought it was amusing when someone was getting some licks in on us. Even though the inmates would get a few licks in, we may get dirty, and the inmates definitely get dirty; in the end — WE WON. WE ALWAYS WON.

Sometimes an inmate would get pissed off for whatever reason, then he became the "I'm gonna get even" inmate. He may have missed his meds or skipped taking some or all of them for a day or two. So now he decided to flood his cell. Stuff the toilet with his clothes, blankets, and bed sheets, and keep the toilet flushing by sticking a plastic 'spork' in the sink handle button that controls the water. There are no faucet handles as we know them, just push buttons. (A spork is a combination spoon and fork made of plastic.) Since there are no drains in the cells, the water ran into the hallway, down the walkway into the other cells, causing those inmates to start raising hell, which added to the stress already happening. The mess this inmate created, as well as the health hazards, could have been the start of more incidents or conflicts with those who were now getting flooded. Those with flooded cells yelled at the one doing the flooding and warned him. Sometimes, that was more than enough to get him to stop, even after ignoring all of our requests. After all, he has to live with the inmates once he gets out of his cell or solitary.

Occasionally, an inmate skipped his meds for a period of time, and then the beast in him became unruly. Medical was notified, and we were instructed to place the inmate in a strap-down cell using leather restraints, where he would be put on a fifteen-minute watch. After this was done, medical staff had to check on the inmate immediately and then, at fifteen-minute intervals, take their vitals and keep a record of everything. There were several occasions when the inmate had to be given a forced sedative to calm him down. A Doctor or an ARNP had to administer this injection and then the inmate had to be monitored by a nurse while he slept it off. It was usually several hours after awakening that it was determined the inmate was 'OK'; he was then returned back to his cell, where he was usually exhausted, and then he slept a lot.

CHARACTERS IN SEGREGATION...

Working in segregation, we had contact with some very colorful and unique individuals. Although we weren't aware of their entire backgrounds, we did have access to their records if need be. So, we knew the basic stories. Some inmates arrived in the middle of the night under cover of darkness, so nobody knew who was there, at least not for a while. This was done for security reasons; if there were enough open cells, we had to segregate them from the other inmates. Segregate in segregation, if possible, in case there were any conflicts with anyone here that we didn't know about. The records could be checked more closely in the morning.

One individual came to us from another state, where he was involved in a prison riot. He actually instigated it and was the ringleader. His original crime was as a motorcycle gang member who did "contract work" for the gang. The murder of his girlfriend was his main charge, for which he received a sentence of twenty-five years with the possibility of parole.

He also did some of his work overseas. He was a very colorful individual who had some great stories to tell, although he didn't divulge any in-depth information. He was a great artist, and he could create anything from Popsicle sticks or matches, sometimes both. He was with us for about seventy days, as other states were wanting to talk to him. He was then transferred to another state. If the inmate did what he said he would do after serving his time, he's living in California. He also did do the entire twenty-five-year sentence.

Another individual we had in segregation was a member of the MENSA society. I only found this out when I delivered some mail to him one day when he received a magazine from MENSA. (It is too lengthy to describe here, but you should look into it.) We had many conversations while he was in segregation, mostly on how he ended up in prison. He once told me, as he chuckled, "Being smart is no excuse for not using common sense." Then he explained how he was talked into his crime by some of his friends, who got him to go along with a plan that turned into an armed robbery. He said he didn't know what was happening, but things went south; everyone was apprehended, and a trial was held. He ended up with five years for his part in someone else's scheme. He got some time off for good behavior and was finally released — never to be heard about again.

Another of the individuals we had, had to go to the hospital to have his appendix removed. He was put in segregation because it was more advantageous to his healing because he could not walk as much, so in segregation, he could lie quietly. But his wound wasn't healing because he kept getting an infection and asking for more pain meds. Medical asked if he could be put in a cell with a camera so we could monitor him. What we noticed was that somehow, he had smuggled in a book of matches, and he was then tearing the matches in half, then tearing off and inserting the match heads into his wound so it wouldn't heal. The wound always maintained a rosy, red color, the same as an infection, and he could complain about the pain. Some individuals do strange things for unknown reasons. When we noticed what he had been doing, medical was notified, his pain meds were discontinued, he healed rather fast, and he was returned to the yard and a regular spot in a dorm.

We had a gang member that came to us from a county jail. He was going to turn state's evidence in a major murder case in the city he was from. It had been a rather large case open for a long time because the detectives couldn't get any solid leads as no one was talking. The detectives handling the case visited the inmate several times in segregation, so nobody knew what was transpiring. Most of these visits were after hours to keep those who didn't have a need to know from seeing or knowing who came and went. Even the inmate janitors were not allowed in during the time the detectives were there. Word from the street to the prison was only a phone call away, so news traveled fast, and information was easily passed. Then the front office found out about a contract hit on him and a reward of $100,000.00 was offered for his demise, the next thing we knew, he suddenly disappeared that night. We never saw him again or knew where he went. Poof. He was just...gone. And we haven't heard his name mentioned again. Not even in the city where he was from. A major case in that city broke several weeks later and arrests were made. It had us wondering, too.

Another guy, who we thought was just having a bad day and for reasons we never found out, decided to knock off the sprinkler head in his cell. Each cell had one in it just in case there was ever a fire in the cell or building. But what he hadn't thought of beforehand was what happens when the water comes out. And that water, sitting in those pipes for a long while, got cold, dank, and stale. Even though the systems were tested, the pipes always had a little water sitting in them. Plus, the shut-off valve was located outside, with the handle under lock and key for safety reasons. Well, lo and behold, he knocks off the head of the sprinkler with his food tray, the alarm rings, and all hell breaks loose. It wakes up the sleeping inmates, who then look out their cell door windows to see what is going on. And the water is flowing. Fast and furious. First, we checked his cell to be sure there was no fire and checked on him. He is OK, except he's all wet; water is everywhere, and he can't hide from it. Even under his bunk, because the water is coming in fast, there is no drain except in the hallway, and the water doesn't run that fast under the door to get out. It also runs into the other cells, and now the other inmates are slowly getting wet and pissed off. People are responding because of the alarm, and the fire and safety officer has to get the key, go outside, unlock the lock, and shut off the valve. Time consuming. And maybe, just maybe he slow walked to shut it off. But it gets done, and the cleanup and a write-up for the inmate begins. Another charge on his record. After his court call date, he was given another thirty days in segregation and was transferred to another prison.

...AND SOME NOT IN SEGREGATION

One of the most colorful characters I met in prison was a very gregarious gentleman who was very small in stature. He had committed the crime of murdering a family member of someone who showed him kindness and even gave him a place to stay for a short period of time. His prison sentence was forever, so he had his mind right. He was also a Vietnam vet who, in the military, had the distinction of being what was then called a "tunnel rat" while in Vietnam. That's how small he was. But he was always on the hustle in prison, trying to get stuff from other inmates in exchange for something or nothing. Always trying to trade up. He had a contagious smile and a chuckle for those that ran into him. He had made the rounds of all the prisons in the state more than once but never wanted a job in any of the facilities. His family usually sent him money each month, although not very much. That's why he was such a hustler. He was surprisingly good at it. He stated many times that he suffered from PTSD (Post Traumatic Stress

Disorder) from his time in Vietnam, although his PTSD could not be confirmed, his military service was. With him being so friendly, who would have believed he was in for murder times two. And his sentence was doing life without. Also known as forever.

One day during a softball game, an inmate misjudged a fly ball that hit him right in the face just above the lip. He had a BIG mustache, which helped cover it up a little. He went to medical, where the medical personnel determined the cut needed to be sewn up, so a trip to the hospital was needed. I was volunteered to take him. As the inmate was getting prepped for his trip to the hospital, his clothes were changed to a jumpsuit, handcuffs, a black box, and shackles were applied while the medical did the paperwork. A black box is a hinged box that goes over the handcuffs and then is secured at the bottom with the belly chain that goes through the box. Then, the chain is secured at the side or back, depending on the inmate's girth, and secured with a padlock. They say it is impossible to get out of, but some inmates say they can. Still, I had never seen anyone do it, so… I was getting a car and weapon ready to transport him to the local hospital. When we arrived at the hospital, we went to a room primarily assigned to inmates. Everything in the room was out of reach and more secure than in a typical exam room. The doctor came in, looked at his lip, and stated it was going to need some stitches, so he would have to numb that first. To which the inmate replied, "Screw it, doc. Just sew it up." The doctor looked at him, at me, then told the nurse, "Ok. Nurse, please get me a suture kit," where he proceeded to sew it up without any numbing or pain meds. It took three stitches on the inside of his lip plus two on the outside. The inmate gave not so much as a flinch, grimace, or whimper. When the doctor was done, the inmate said he was ready to go back to prison, to which he added, "I hope someone saved dinner for me." Hell, it hurt me just to watch.

Tattoos in prison are very common. Many get some on the street as they grow up. Some get tattooed in between stints in prison. Still some others get tattooed while in prison. Those are the worst kind because of the unsanitary conditions from using the motor from CD players to rigging up batteries to provide the power to the machines that run the needles. These needles are usually made from paper clips that are sharpened to a point by rubbing them on the concrete walls or floors of their cells. The ink they use comes from the print shop or just an ordinary ink pen. YUP, printing ink in various colors smuggled out to be sold, bought or traded on the yard. All for a price, of course. After all, it is prison. Ya' gotta have a hustle to survive.

There was one new inmate who came in with numerous tattoos. Upon arrival in prison, all inmates are processed, new photos taken, and any major identifying marks or tattoos are then noted as well as photographed. Noted. This was for easier identification. But the one tattoo he had that stood out, was around his neck. It looked like perforated or dotted lines going around his neck, with the exception of an open spot in the front, just below his Adam's apple. Written there were the words ---- "CUT HERE" ----. We thought it was funny and so did he.

Another individual who came to us was a return guest. He had made parole and found himself a decent job. But he was later terminated from that job. He never said what happened at work, but he got pissed off and decided he wanted to be a

NINJA, or he thought that he was one, dressed up all in black — black trench coat, face mask, and gloves. Hidden under his trench coat, he had a few weapons and a long rifle. He then went to a local university, where he started shooting. He fired at no one in particular, just walking around shooting in a building. Police were called, and a standoff began.

The standoff lasted several hours when he finally surrendered. His explanation later was he was just pissed off. This inmate was always a troublemaker in prison with his constant filing of lawsuits against the Warden, staff members, kitchen workers, and anyone who he didn't like. He was always a pain; even some of the other inmates didn't care for all his disruptions. When he was transferred to another state, everyone was pleased as punch that he finally left.

Then there were some individuals who tried to make themselves more attractive while in prison, who should have been at KCIW but did not complete the transition process from male to female. There was a particular individual whose crimes were robbery and theft, for which he received five years. He stated that he did his crimes so he could pay for his transition operations. I guess that didn't work out well. But when he finally made parole, he was picked up in a limousine that had an entourage in the back. What a way to go. These individuals would use all the tricks that they had in their repertoire. Pool chalk from the pool tables for making eyeliner was the cosmetic of choice. It came in two colors, blue and green. For blush and lipstick, this was accomplished by using powdered drink mix in various flavors/colors that were mixed with a little water to make a paste, which was then used to enhance their "beauty" and make themselves more colorful. For the inmates who were interested in these kinds of people, they found these folks attractive and impressive.

Another makeup trick that was used was the colored drawing pencils, which were sold in the inmate's commissary and used primarily for making greeting cards that were "sold" on the yard. Of course, when the guards saw this, we had to tell them to go clean up because some inmates just couldn't handle it and wanted to pursue things a little further than they should. This, in turn, led to more confrontations. So, to avoid that attention, inmates usually arranged things at night, behind closed doors, when nobody or we could see who the love bug bit.

Remember this: that when you are looking for a "girlfriend" today, so is somebody else. Just like back home, it leads to jealousy, jealousy leads to confrontation, and confrontation leads to segregation.

When everyone comes to prison as they get processed, all their property is inventoried, and things that they are not allowed to have or cannot keep are set aside so they can get mailed home. Next, they get a haircut. Not a bald style one but a close cut, then given a shower with a medicinal soap to kill bugs, lice, etc. After all that, a new photo is taken for their records with their new ID number or for return customers, an old number if it's still available for use. I remember a young man who came to the prison in the late eighties. He was processed like all others. His haircut was done, and he then proceeded to let his hair grow while he was at that prison. He let it grow like a guy on a popular TV show named Bart. He kept it that way for his entire stay, which was about three years. He kept it neat, and it grew really nice. His hair eventually reached about six inches tall, and he kept it well-trimmed.

When in the yard, he had a certain swagger about him, like he was the king of the yard. His favorite activity in the yard was gambling. He would make books on any sporting event or activity on the yard, or any sports event going on outside like major league baseball, football, or basketball. He covered them all. He was really good so it was extremely hard to catch him. Many searches of him or his cell revealed nothing. No bet slips and no detailed lists of any bets by individuals. If he had them on his person, we never found them. Everyone knew he was guilty, but catching him with the evidence or proving it were two different things; he was never caught. His yard nickname was 'Black Bart' due to his iconic hairstyle and his being African-American.

PRECAUTIONS WE TOOK

Gloves, gloves, and more gloves. We always carried more than a few pairs on us. They were always available, so we used them. Also, hand sanitizer. We all had a small bottle along with extra gloves in an extra pouch on the utility belt.

When someone got locked up in segregation, after they were processed in and medical was done with the screening, we all had questions for the nurses about who just came in. We were curious, just in case we had to do a cell entry or come into closer contact with them, and we wanted to know if we were at risk. This could mean the difference between a routine procedure and planning for the worst. But because of the HIPPA laws (Health Insurance Portability and Accountability Act), Medical couldn't tell us much. When we would ask, the staff always added, "If you see me put on a mask or gown as well as gloves, I suggest you do the same." That was all we needed to know, so we made notes on everyone's segregation paperwork. We always took precautions, just in case to try to stay safe. The inmate janitors even took precautions. Sometimes, the janitors found out or knew important details before us because of the living quarters and the internal inmate gossip line.

Another tool that we used was called "the Restraint Chair." It was utilized when an unruly inmate needed a "time out," but the incident was not quite bad enough for a strap-down cell. When this special technique was used, the inmate was seated in the restraint chair with the seat being a deep V where the buttocks go. The angle was about thirty–five degrees, so it was very hard to stand without assistance from someone else or by using the armrests. When seated, the individual was secured with straps at each wrist and ankle as well as around his chest, but it was designed to not restrict breathing, just normal moving. The chair weighed about eighty pounds but could fit through a standard thirty-inch-wide door and hold up to a four hundred fifty-pound person. A spit hood or mask was usually applied to prevent any spitting on or at us. The mask did not hinder their breathing; it just prevented spitting since their mouth was covered. A protective football-style helmet was available if the inmate started banging their head on the back of the restraint chair, even if the chair was padded ever so slightly. Although many tried to overturn the chair, no one ever succeeded. We could only keep the person in the restraint chair for a short time, not to exceed three hours, and then they had to be checked or rechecked by medical. Hopefully, by this time, the inmate had calmed down enough so we could release him from the chair and get him back to his cell to resume a normal daily routine.

Frequent hand washing, especially with sanitizer, was foremost on our minds, so we all practiced this a lot every day. Most officers carried their own small bottles with them every day. One cannot be too careful. We didn't spare the sanitizer when we were using it.

Being careful extended beyond just ourselves. If we had an open drink that we didn't keep an eye on or left it unobserved for any length of time, especially if inmates were around, we threw it out. You never know if something was put in it. There were no taking chances, even if it was full. Trust no one.

FREQUENTLY ASKED QUESTIONS

During my twelve years of working for the Kentucky Department of Corrections, I have seen a lot of inmates come and go. I knew the possibility existed that I would see some of them on the street again; it was real, and I did sometimes. When we did see each other, it was always very cordial. Hello, how are you, hope that all is well with you and then goodbye. Most didn't want to engage in a long conversation, but the few that did all stated that they were fine, staying out of trouble, and had no hard feelings because they knew I (we) had a job to do. Then after the brief interaction, we went our separate ways. I always wished them continued success.

Many of the people that I meet and talk to socially, i.e., friends or people I see on the golf course, at a ball game, or in any of the normal social situations where we made small talk, inevitably got around to what everyone did for a living. It was just casual conversations in general to help pass the time.

Whenever I mentioned that I was a Correctional Officer and worked in a medium-security prison in the state, the questions came in no particular order. But everyone wanted to know what it was like to be locked up with murderers, rapists, and thugs of all kinds.

When people heard where I worked, they thought it was funny to say things like, "Don't drop the soap." It's not like we hadn't heard that one before. Even though guards don't use the showers, people thought it was hilarious.

Questions often started like this:

Did I ever get attacked or have to fight someone, and what was the outcome?

Yes, I did, but not many times. Occasionally, an inmate, in front of others, will do something crazy like attack an officer. They'll take a swing at us, grab us, and wrestle with us. It's usually in front of other inmates, and it's done to prove a point to everyone watching. They want to try and show whoever is around that they are a badass and have no fear. It also sends a message that they aren't scared of conflict, so don't mess with them. We each got a few licks in, but no serious injuries happened, and in the end, they lost and went to the hole or were transferred to another prison. After an inmate got out of the hole, they were just like all the rest. They usually apologized and were very contrite, except for the one guy.

This inmate attacked me while in segregation. We swapped a few punches and tussled on the floor, but there were no major injuries. The next day he was transferred to another facility, so our paths never crossed again. I still don't know why he decided to attack me, but maybe he just wanted a transfer, which was his way of expediting it.

Was I ever scared?

Yes, especially in the beginning because I didn't know what to expect. It takes a lot of self-confidence to work there, and it's something they can't teach at the academy. The first scare I had was when I was working in the chow hall. That's where my first confrontation occurred with an inmate who was about six foot six and two hundred ninety pounds. He was staring me down to see what I would do. He was also testing me to see if I would give in, but I knew that if I did, I would never be able to hold my own with or against any inmate on the yard. After several minutes, he nodded and went on his way. I never had any more problems with him again. And if you are scared, try not to let it show. Anybody who says that they are not scared is lying to you.

Did prison change me?

Yes, it changes everyone in one way or another. We mostly become aware that the inmates are also humans who made mistakes, even though some of their crimes were despicable. Our job was not to judge. That had already been done by a jury of their peers. We also learned to take what was said to us by the inmates with a grain of salt.

Do all inmates claim that they are innocent?

Not all do, but some do. Even if they are not innocent, in their minds, they are, and they spend a lot of time in the law library looking for an out or an appeal. But almost all are guilty and justifiably convicted in a court of law.

Are there any preconceived notions about prison?

There sure are. Some people think that all the inmates are locked up all day and get out for only an hour or two a day. Some people even think that we carry guns or batons with us, but we don't. Those weapons could be taken from us by the inmates who would use them on us or another inmate. There are also a lot of good and enjoyable opportunities for the inmates if they want to take advantage of them. And with cable TV in each cell available for each inmate, to some, life is good.

Did I ever feel sorry for anyone? (Sympathy)

Yes, on one occasion, after hearing their story and checking the records to find out why they did what they did it, I was sympathetic. Of course, not all records tell a complete story, but the basics are there. We had to learn the difference between sympathy, empathy, and compassion for what and why they committed their crime.

Do prisons work?

Generally, they work for what they were designed for. As for the days of 'lock 'em up and throw away the key, that's very archaic in most instances, and it is not a great deterrent to crime. But it is needed and does need to be used in some cases. It's better and cheaper in the long run to rehabilitate inmates and to teach them better ways to run and control their lives when their time is served. Some were locked up long before computers, cellphones, and modern electronics were so abundant, and some older inmates knew nothing about how to use the technology. Teach them before they get out, and show them how to function in a modern world to reduce the recidivism rate.

Does rehab work?

It does for those who are willing to put forth the effort to make changes or have a desire to stay out of prison. Most prisons today have programs called something like 'prison to the streets' to help acclimate the inmates when they are getting out. These programs teach them about computers, cell phones, ATM machines, etc. Some inmates, however, just don't care and think that a life of easy crime is worth it or better than conforming to the rules of society. That's why they keep returning to prison. Or some are there so long they become institutionalized and have no desire to be free.

What is the difference between minimum, medium, and max security?

Each inmate is rated on various items. Such as whether he is likely to re-offend. Did they commit a violent crime? Do they seem to have a strong support base at home? What is their mental status at the time of the crime or their current status after receiving their sentence? Based on a score when he is evaluated after being sentenced to prison, a prisoner might be determined to need a different level of incarceration. This is usually done at the intake or reception prison before being sent to a more permanent home.

There are many factors that go into this score, including the type of crime or crimes committed, the age(s) of the victim(s), and the violence of the crime committed. How likely are the criminals to recommit another crime? Psychological evaluations that were conducted before arriving at the prison or will be conducted shortly after arrival are tools used in this evaluation.

Minimum security means they could be eligible to do their time in county jail, have outside job details while there (cleaning highway trash, etc.), or need less close supervision.

Medium means that there is more of a threat than can be managed with minimum security and requires closer or enhanced supervision. These inmates are generally not eligible for outside details or work release under any supervision. Although their crimes are bad, they usually do not include any type of capital crime charge. (Murder, rape, arson.)

Maximum means close supervision with no access to any outside work assignments and the inmate must be escorted by two officers whenever they are transported outside of the facility for any reason. The sentences they receive are generally longer, and there is not much chance for parole due to the violent nature of their crime. Most are life terms with little chance of lowering their custody score, but it is possible with continuous good behavior to change their score. Most of these inmates are with convictions that include life sentences. Death row, for the states that have it, is maximum security. This status can only be changed, usually by the governor of the state or by the President.

Why do most people go to prison?

My personal belief is that a breakdown in society's rules as they become laxer, plus a lack of a strong home structure, contributes to their downfall. With little or no parental guidance, they learn the street ways of life and fall under the influence of those around them, most of whom do not have a home structure either. With little or no completed education, the thought of easy money comes into play. Some people even have a notion that society owes them everything because they don't have it while someone else does, and they want to have it too without working for it.

Do inmates become institutionalized?

Yes, after many, many years in, that's all they come to know and become accustomed to, so without much interaction with the modern conveniences of today's outside world, they don't comprehend all that is available and normal outside of prison. Some come to know and realize this is their new normal. Think back to the movie "Shawshank Redemption," where several inmates get out and go to live in the boarding house. They can't adjust to not being told what to do, when to do it, and where to go. They are used to the direction and structure they had in prison.

Have I ever received any direct threats?

Yes. There was one inmate who said that when he got out, he was going to kill me because I did a write-up on him that caused him to spend some time in the hole, and he also lost some good time, thereby meaning that his sentence would not be cut short by the parole board. The adjustment committee took some of his good time because of his write-up, which I believe was sixty days. I reported it to the front office, other official reports were made, and memos were placed in his permanent record, just in case, but I retired first before he made parole. Even today I always watch my surroundings and make sure no one is following me. I don't put my guard down until I know I wasn't being followed.

Did I ever meet any dangerous inmates?

It depends on what is meant by dangerous. Dangerous on the outside? Yes, there were a few who were considered extremely dangerous. They were never going to get out, and the crimes they committed were horrendous and grotesque. These inmates were transferred from prison to prison about every nine months, so they couldn't get too comfortable. We also had a few major gang leaders from out of state. On the inside, dangerous meant they needed to be watched closer than the other inmates. We knew who they were, and we were always aware when in close proximity to them. It was about watching your back and your partners' back. There were also the ones who we knew had previously attacked staff in any institution.

Were there any 'famous' inmates that we had?

We had several. Two were former professional football players, and one of them played for a team that went to the Super Bowl. He did participate in the game but had no major impact. And no, we didn't ask for autographs, but we had their signatures on many official prison documents. We also couldn't divulge who they were.

Was I ever offered a bribe?

Yes, on several occasions, especially while working in the visiting room. There were offers of money if I could extend their visits longer, especially during the holidays, like Thanksgiving, Christmas, and New Year's Day, when the visiting room was at the overfull point, and someone had to go. Visits were always conducted on a first-in-first-out basis. When it was crowded, visits were limited to a max of two hours to keep things moving when more visitors were waiting. The money that was offered to me ranged from twenty dollars to fifty dollars. These bribe offers came from the wives, girlfriends, and mothers. All for a little extra time. It was usually from the ones who drove the furthest.

There was one lady who, when she visited, was almost always the first one there. She never stayed longer than two hours. One day, we asked her why she was always the first to visit and stayed such a short time even when it wasn't busy. She stated that she had to go to the other two prisons in the same area (there were three prisons located near where I was) so she could visit her husband and another son, who were in the other institutions. The visiting times varied from prison to prison.

Wow! Three from the same family in three different prisons. What a family life. I wonder what the dinner conversation will be like when there's a family reunion.

Did I ever develop any prejudices towards any of the inmates?

Yes, I did. It was towards the ones that committed crimes against kids and the elderly. These were the most defenseless and most vulnerable of all victims. I was especially bothered by the sex crimes. But still, you have to treat them all the same. And you try to keep your feelings in check and not let them show.

What was the most depressing thing I saw at work?

Watching someone die while performing CPR on them. Even though they are inmates, it still gets to you. It's the human side of everyone. There were several inmates who died while I was employed, and it got to the officers who were involved, even if we all tried to hide it. If it doesn't, then there's got to be something wrong with you.

Do people really hide stuff up their butt?

Yes, they do. When tobacco was allowed in prison, it was the number one item smuggled and packed away. Then, there are betting slips and the master debt lists. These were always kept separate for obvious reasons in case either was found. But it happens more frequently than you can imagine. It's commonly called a prison pocket.

What happens to cop killers in prison?

It depends on your state and whether it's a federal or state facility. In some prisons, these inmates are usually held in high regard among the other inmates because they got one of 'them', and the inmates usually give these guys a wide berth with dibs on a lot of things. Remember, it's the game of cops vs robbers. Cop killers are considered the apex of inmates. On the other hand, child molesters are at the lowest spectrum and get beat up quite often. The lowest of the low.

Do inmates and officers get along?

Both sides understand that this is their current lot in life, although only one of us can leave at any time we want, while the other cannot. It's easier to go along to get along. It's a two-way street. Respecting each other's boundaries, and the ability to be pleasant, but they'll never be beer-drinking buddies.

Is there a lot of contraband in prison?

It depends on what you mean by a lot. Any contraband is too much, but it's impossible to keep it all out. It comes in, in many ways, and sadly to say, as long as there are dirty correctional officers or other staff, there will always be contraband getting in. The inmates, family, and friends try to think of ways to get it in, and we try to figure out how to keep it out.

What is the difference between a concurrent sentence and a consecutive sentence?

A concurrent sentence is one given by the court for crimes committed. IE: If you receive three sentences of five years each to run concurrently, it means that they all run together. So, it's basically a total of five years to do, not fifteen. (Less parole unless otherwise stated.)

When a sentence is given by the judge, and it says that you have (IE;) three five-year sentences to be served consecutively. It means that you must serve five years on the first sentence, then start on the second five-year sentence, and then start on the third five-year sentence for a total of fifteen years. (Less parole unless otherwise stated.) Or a time-period specified by the judge.

These details are usually worked out ahead of time between the prosecution and defense attorneys with approval from the judge. The time served is also subject to any parole conditions handed down by the courts.

That is a glimpse inside a prison with all its good and bad. There are many more stories to be told from many different lock-up facilities, jails, and prisons, and I hope that my fellow officers will tell them one day.

STAY SAFE
AND LIFE GOES ON

Epilogue
BEING A CORRECTIONAL OFFICER
CAN DESTROY YOUR LIFE.

As an officer, you are placed in a disease environment and, at times, a violent world of pain and despair. Shrouded from the good and the innocent, from the love, happiness, calm, and quiet everyone desires and needs. You are often secluded with society's worst, attempting to correct the behavior of those who, in most cases, don't want to be corrected. In most cases, we don't correct their behavior. Our jobs were to keep them safe, mostly from each other and safe from themselves.

The outside world does not care about the unseen world of the officers. The uninformed pretend the brutal world of corrections doesn't exist. The politicians in charge turn their backs until something bad happens. At that point, the questions are being asked, and fingers are pointed, often at the officers, while saying that it's our fault for not doing our job correctly.

Slowly, the officers become desensitized and withdrawn from their family and friends. On the outside of the walls, there is nobody to talk to. People don't understand because your life is usually shrouded and hidden from the public. When you go out, you often find yourself sitting at the back of the room with your back to the wall facing the door. A loud bang has you jumping, fearing the worst. When going out, you always want to face the door to see what or who is coming in.

Corrections take its toll on your health and your mind. Eating away at you from the inside out. The public should think about its correction officers and the job they perform to protect you and your family from the unseen. Pray that they stay safe so they can return home to their loved ones unharmed. Think about your correction officers and how their lives are affected by this hidden world. Thank them for all that they give up for you and your family. In closing, think about their sacrifices.

AUTHOR UNKNOWN, BUT WITH MANY THANKS TO A FELLOW C/O.

To paraphrase what General Eisenhower once said. "If you want total security — go to prison. There you are fed, clothed, and given your meds and medical attention. The only thing you lack is FREEDOM".

DON'T DO THE CRIME IF YOU
CAN'T DO THE TIME.

Printed in the United States
by Baker & Taylor Publisher Services

Printed in the United States
by Baker & Taylor Publisher Services